Clergy and Clients

CLERGY and CLIENTS

*The Practice of
Pastoral Psychotherapy*

RONALD R. LEE, PHD

A CROSSROAD BOOK

THE SEABURY PRESS : NEW YORK

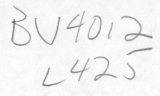

1980
The Seabury Press
815 Second Avenue / New York, N.Y. 10017

Library of Congress Catalog Card Number: 80-50-606
ISBN: 0-8164-0115-2

Acknowledgments

I wish to thank:
my mentors—Carroll Wise, Carl Christensen,
  Alfred Flarsheim, Thomas Klink, Leo Thomas
  and Bernard Greene, for helping me see the
  possibilities of pastoral psychotherapy,

my clients, students and colleagues—for the basic
  material for the book,

my therapists—Vernon Clark and Richard Chessick,
  for the tools of a depression-free life,

my family—for its sustaining love,

and—Eleanor West, Donna Cacharelis and Mary,
  my wife, for typing the manuscript.

Contents

Introduction

The concept of a pastor functioning as a psychotherapist is of recent origin. While the church has had a tradition of healing since biblical times, the actual conducting of psychotherapy by pastors has evolved mainly because of the influence of the theories and methods of Sigmund Freud and his successors. In this book the term pastor means a religious leader, such as a priest, rabbi, or minister, who has normally been ordained or set aside in some other special way. Psychotherapy in this text denotes treatment rendered in scheduled sessions where through interpretation and insight, significant changes occur in the beliefs, feelings, and behavior of the person seeking help. Where the term pastoral therapy or pastoral psychotherapy is used, it means psychotherapy conducted by a pastor.

The text is aimed at being helpful to different kinds of readers. Of prime concern are graduate students in pastoral therapy who are generally fully trained pastors in their late 20s or early 30s with experience in parish ministry. Their person-centered ministry has challenged them to seek specialized training to help persons whose needs are far greater than traditional pastoral care can meet.

Another group that should find the text of particular interest are parish pastors who want to understand what takes place when they make a referral to a therapeutic specialist. They might also read the text out of a desire to improve their abilities at making a referral or for conducting short-term counseling (pastoral care). Such pastors generally want to be of maximum help to the members of their church but as generalists. This is often because they recognize the value of, and prefer, a multifaceted ministry. The choice by pastors who have the background and ability to undertake specialized training in pastoral therapy not to do so is generally deliberate and is usually made because they value the breadth of the generalist's work. For them, there is more joy in helping many persons to good resources than in working in depth with the few. Without generalists, many people would not make it to the therapeutic specialist.

The pastoral therapy specialist should also find the text useful. While there are many excellent texts in pastoral counseling (Hiltner 1949, Wise 1951, Johnson 1953, Oates 1959, Jackson 1975) there are none that focus on pastoral psychotherapy, especially on its technical aspects. Most trained pastoral therapists have used texts from psychiatry, psychology, social work, and counseling. This book, however, is written by a pastor for pastors. It seeks to explain the basis of psychotherapy, illustrating by examples which came out of the author's last 15 years of practice in church and seminary offices. Much of the material also came from his emotional and intellectual struggles in helping people he supervised to understand the processes of psychotherapy as these unfolded with their clients. And some information included stemmed from didactic seminars he conducted. While the theoretical ideas elaborated are not of an advanced technical nature, nor original, it is hoped that, because these ideas are rooted in experience, they will bring clarity and freshness to the understanding of psychotherapy conducted by a pastor.

Also, counselors and therapists who are not pastors may find this text of some interest. If the number of counseling education students who cross-register from university to seminary classes in pastoral therapy is any indication, neophyte counselors and therapists may find the book, because of its practical emphasis, a good introduction to their later work. Experienced mental health professionals wanting to sample the work of pastoral therapists may also want to read it. Of course, the book represents only one person's position and the theoretical orientations in the pastoral therapy movement are as diverse as those in its secular counterparts. Even so, the text gives some indication as to the nature of the work being undertaken by many of the 2,000 members of the American Association of Pastoral Counselors. While much of their work is short term and crisis oriented, there tends to be a myth in mental health circles that this short-term counseling, or pastoral care, is all pastoral counselors are capable of doing. Hopefully, this text will correct this oversimplified position.

Another group that may want to read the book are persons who are undergoing or contemplating undergoing psychotherapy. For two years the manuscript of the book was made available to students taking pastoral care or pastoral therapy classes, and many of these, in psychotherapy at the time, took the trouble to see the author and indicate ways in which the material gave them insights into their own therapy. While there may sometimes be difficulties because persons in therapy can use the book to reinforce intellectual defenses and avoid painful issues, this danger can be dealt with by skilled therapists. Many have testified that the text enabled them to make a decision to undergo therapy. Perhaps the experience of these students may not be easily replicated in society as a whole, nevertheless reading these pages may inspire many, who would otherwise draw back from the life-significant experience that psychotherapy can be, with sufficient desire to seek therapeutic change.

Before turning to the main chapters, some further clarification of the definition of psychotherapy is necessary. This is because the term is often used to cover a wide range of therapeutic activities, with counseling at one end of the continuum, and psychoanalysis at the other. In this book, psychotherapy is meant to cover a narrower range of therapeutic activities somewhere between the two. Psychotherapy as used here covers three specific types: supportive (Gill 1951, Wolberg 1954), brief (Lewin 1970), and intensive uncovering (Fromm-Reichmann 1950, Langs 1973 and 1974, Chessick 1974). All these types of psychotherapy are considered pastoral therapy if the therapy is conducted by an identified pastor. Supportive pastoral therapy attempts to strengthen the clients' (ego) defenses, bring emotional reequilibrium, and relieve symptoms. In brief pastoral therapy the aim is to achieve some insight, modify the client's punitive (sadistic) conscience, and achieve some limited behavior change, without attempting to alter the basic personality structure with its constellation of defenses. In intensive, uncovering pastoral therapy the goal is to promote change in the core character structure through insight into the reasons for repeated patterns of behavior (repetition compulsion), through insight into conflicts and defenses, and through continuing with the client until these insights and changes are worked through.

The pastoral therapy discussed in this book follows no one particular school. It is broadly psychodynamic within the psychoanalytic tradition, taking the position that it is more important to understand the process of psychotherapy from one frame of reference as thoroughly as possible, than to have a smattering of a dozen different theories. The process of psychotherapy falls naturally into three main phases called the beginning, middle, and termination. An understanding of these has helped form the material of the book. Chapters 2, 3, and 4 cover the initial phase; chapters 5 and 6, the middle phase; and chapter 7, the termination phase.

There is a need to define pastoral care in contrast to pastoral therapy (Wise 1966). Through visiting people in their home, giving premarital sessions, dealing with emergencies, taking sacraments to the sick and shut-ins, facilitating grief, visiting persons in-hospital, and making referrals, the pastor practices the time-honored role of care agent. While a lot of healing takes place as a result of this work and therefore could be considered pastoral therapy in a broad sense, it is not what is being referred to as pastoral therapy in this book because such a broad usage introduces too much confusion. In pastoral care situations, if appointments are made, they are generally just for once, or are irregularly scheduled over a period of time, and the sessions are generally short. Often contacts are made in informal situations with the pastor's availability and accessibility being two of the pastor's best assets. Such pastoral care work is sometimes referred to as pastoral counseling, but as counseling used so broadly loses some of its meaning, this text will use pastoral care or pastoral therapy as defined and try to avoid the term counseling altogether.

Throughout each chapter there tends to be an interaction taking place between pastoral therapy on the one hand, and general practice, including pastoral care, on the other. This is because each can contribute to the other. From personal experience the author is aware that training and practice in psychotherapy has improved his ability to be a pastoral care agent. This is reflected in chapter 8, where referral is used as an example of pastoral care that has been helped and informed by the practice of pastoral therapy. On the other hand, experience in pastoral care can be a tremendous asset in the practice of pastoral therapy. Those with good pastoral care training and experience generally find it easier to develop a working alliance (chapter 5) with clients, and often have a better sensitivity in working with "sicker" clients, such as those with a "borderline" diagnosis. (The term borderline is used here to designate persons who are more dysfunctional than neurotics but better able to function in the world than schizophrenics.)

The contribution that pastoral care can make to an understanding of pastoral therapy is delineated in several chapters where a theoretical point in pastoral therapy is illustrated by referring to experiences in general practice. This may help those pastors without an experience of the therapeutic relationship, either as therapist or client, to identify with the point better. A risk in doing this is that the text may sometimes appear a little disjointed, even irrelevant, if the reader has experienced psychotherapy firsthand. Yet, where possible there has been an attempt to draw parallels between the structural forces at work in both pastoral psychotherapy and general ministry. The assumption made here is that at a basic level these structures are very similar, if not the same. Trying to help persons raises similar issues whether it is attempted by a neighbor over a cup of coffee, a pastor in performing pastoral duties, or a psychotherapist in a formal setting. Questions relating to the way a person seeks help, of evaluation of the person's character, structure of the relationship, alliance, distortion of reality, and termination of the relationship always arise, whether the person trying to help is aware of these questions or not.

Furthermore, all helping relationships seem to have the phases mentioned earlier—beginning, middle, and termination. The disadvantage of informal attempts at helping from the point of view of educating the helper is that the issues related to the initial, middle, and termination phases are raised and settled so quickly that there is virtually no time to reflect on and correct them during the process. The initial, middle, and termination phases that take place in 50 sessions of psychotherapy, for example, offer a leisurely educational advantage that the quick shifts in a five-minute conversation cannot. Corrections can be made in pastoral therapy training through supervision of the therapist between sessions with a client. Pastoral care tends to be hit-or-miss, with the main learning coming as post facto analysis. On the other hand, pastoral care forces the helper into the position of having to make decisions and then live with them. Thus, the position taken here is not that pastoral therapy is a better way to learn pastoral care, but that it adds a dimension which contributes a great deal.

The need by any pastor wishing to conduct psychotherapy for personal psychotherapy and extensive supervision by a qualified therapist is particularly stressed in the conclusion of the book. In the case of those wishing to be pastoral therapy specialists, there is no way that a book such as this one can be any more than a preparation for the training that personal psychotherapy and years of supervision can provide.

1 : Presentation

The way a person requests help is of great importance to the skilled practitioner of pastoral therapy. This is because the first few moments of the initial interaction contain a great deal of diagnostic material uncluttered by details and generally magnified as a result of anxiety. How the person consciously and unconsciously presents herself or himself as well as her or his problem, invariably reveals major coping (defensive) behavior. Where this behavior is extreme or in-appropriate it will reveal what is called "presenting transference."

Transference, as discussed in chapter six, consists of distortions in a relationship because of early infant or childhood memories. Not all behavior in the initial meeting with the pastoral therapist is of this distorted quality. However, because all presenting behavior contains derivatives of transference distortions, the therapists, through careful attention to these derivatives, can be prepared for the transferences that will develop during the course of the pastoral therapy. Seeing transference distortions during these initial moments is of immense value because they are less likely to be reactions to the behavior of the therapist than at any other time in the relationship.

From experience, the author has found it extremely difficult to teach beginning pastoral therapists the minute signs of possible transference in the presenting relationship. It has boggled many a neophyte's mind when predictions about diagnosis and course of therapy made by a skilled therapist using a detailed clinical description of only the first few minutes of the initial session are confirmed by clinical material of later sessions, known only to the neophyte. It may appear like intuition or magic, but it isn't. Such predictions are the result of a lot of careful observation of initial minutiae and the use of a simplified principle of convergence. (Campbell and Fisk, 1959).

One of the reasons why neophytes find signs of presenting transference difficult to notice is the "Catch 22" situation in which they find themselves. On the one hand, signs of presenting transference are often missing in the written material they submit for supervision, making it difficult to learn from supervision. On the other hand, until they know what to look for in any systematic way, only a fraction of the data pointing to transference in the presenting relationship will be noted and included. Generally, a skilled supervisor can help a neophyte recall some material pertinent to presenting transference, especially if the supervision is scheduled soon after the therapy session. Such recalled material is generally incomplete, yet it helps expand the student's sensitivity to the behavior being sought, and leads to more reporting of material on presenting relationship in later supervisory sessions. The reality is that initial interacting goes far too quickly for a nervous beginner to note very much unless she or he is prepared.

Based on supervision of such students, the author has found a lack of awareness of material in at least two or three of the following areas in much of the written material presented for supervision.

1. Way the person contacted the therapist to make an appointment
2. Way the person behaved
3. First words spoken by the person
4. Way the person appeared
5. Problem that brought the person to seek help

These areas are noted for emphasis and diagnostic purposes. In actuality, the client presents herself or himself in a gestalt (totality) to the therapist. As a means of sharpening a neophyte's awareness of this gestalt, increased attention to the above areas has been successful with many of the author's supervisees.

This chapter not only is meant to alert the student of pastoral therapy to the material of presenting transference, but is also intended for the general practitioner of ministry who wishes to sharpen skills in pastoral care. In conducting such care, the pastor is generally without the benefit of tests and is often ignorant of the history of the person seeking help.

Always available to the pastor, without the asking, is material from the presenting relationship if only the pastor has the training to understand and use it. True, pastors can get to know a lot about members of their congregation if both pastor and members stay in a locality long enough. Such knowledge of family and/or personal history can be extremely important in the caring work of a pastor. However, the image of the shepherd knowing her or his sheep is an ideal one. Realistically, as modern society and ministry become more mobile, such intimate detailed knowledge of families is increasingly missing, and sketchy at best. Those doing pastoral care, in urban situations especially, have been forced to rely more heavily on diagnostic skills based on the way a person seeking help presents to the pastor, than did pastors of previous generations.

When persons contact a pastor, whatever the contact, they expect a warm caring attitude. The pastor, therefore, is confronted with the problem of how to express care, yet evaluate through the person's words and behavior, her or his needs, and then move that person towards utilizing the appropriate resources. What the author has learned from personal experience is that the process of reading a write-up of the presenting relationship, essential in pastoral therapy, can be enormously helpful in a pastoral care situation. The following, is an example of a write-up for supervision, done in such a way as to outline the areas mentioned earlier. The headings are included for reiteration; in actual practice, they are left out.

Write-up No. 1
   Identifying Information (disguised)
     Session: No. 1
     Date: January 19, 1979
     Place: St. John's Church, Ballarat, Victoria
     Client: Mrs. Smith
           2264 Seabury Street
           Naperville, Illinois 60001
           Phone: Work—GA 7-9388
                   Home—HO 2-1200
     Pastor: Tom Jones
   Contact: A parishioner mentioned Mrs. Smith, a new neighbor, as a prospect for church membership. I called on Mrs. Smith, told her of the church program, where the church was located, and invited her

to attend. Six months later Mrs. Smith came to the parsonage without an appointment.

Description: Mrs. Smith is an attractive woman, possibly in her early 40s, of average height and weight. She was dressed in dark slacks, flat shoes, a plain blouse, and a light-blue jacket. Her weathered face had a tired look around the eyes. The line of her mouth slanted down as she spoke in a quiet voice.

Initial Behavior: Mrs. Smith seemed hesitant and nervous and glanced over her shoulder up the street before coming into the house. She took a seat on the edge of the couch near the door of my study and sat with her hands folded and legs drawn together. She seemed very uncomfortable. She wrung her hands as she leaned forward and spoke.

Initial Words: "I want to talk to you about a problem that has been bothering me. I trust you, as a minister, and don't want anyone to know, especially my husband."

Presenting Complaint or Problem: Mrs. Smith stated that her husband was seeing another woman. She didn't think she could cope with it much longer.

This write-up was not selected for any special reason except that it was submitted by a pastor under supervision. Many questions could be raised about the material. However, a key question is whether the woman is requesting support, or whether she is requesting treatment for a paranoid personality where she projects her fears as though they were real. Although at this point it is not known what she wants, the presenting material has already helped raise some essential hypotheses and should alert the pastor to look for clues in the material that will follow. In the rest of this chapter material that relates to each of these headings will be discussed.

Identifying Information

This is easy to forget, so as soon as it is reasonably possible the person's address and telephone number should be taken down if it's not already on file. Many attempts at help have been derailed at the beginning because the pastor became sick or had to cancel for an emergency and had no way of contacting the person except by a note on the church door.

Contact

The first task for a pastor, at the point of contact, is to ascertain if the person is requesting personal help, and if so, whether she or he is the one to attempt it. This is where ministry is different from many of the helping professions. Pastors can't assume that they are the best persons to render help in every case. If the answer to these two questions seems to be yes, the pastor's goal, at the contact stage, generally is to make an appointment.

Persons contact the pastor in many ways: at the door after worship, along church corridors, by mail or telephone, on the street, or in an elevator, to mention a few. These contacts can mean anything from a few moments of social chit-chat, a discussion of some organization details of a coming church event, or a serious request for personal help. Because of the pastor's role, she or he may be contacted for just about anything. The pastor's historic availability is an asset because persons may make a contact that otherwise would not have been made. But the pastor's very openness can be a liability unless she or he develops a method of sorting out the nature of the request and giving the request for personal help the time and freedom from distraction necessary to explore its dimensions. An appointment enables this to happen; making an appointment is generally the goal of the pastor when a contact is made involving personal help.

As indicated earlier, it is not always clear if a person, in contacting a pastor, is actually making a request for help. This may be because the request for time from the pastor can be indirect, possibly out of fear of rejection. It may be that the request is made unconsciously, and unless the pastor senses this with her or his "third ear" and suggests talking about it further, the real need doesn't surface. Whatever the reason for a subtle approach by the person, the more skill the pastor develops, the more she or he will discover meaning and purpose behind many of the transactions that occur in a seemingly innocent contact.

Effective pastoral care does not require a formal appointment. The author knows from personal experience, and has heard of many cases of effective pastoral care done "on the hoof." However, the point is that for effective pastoral care, an appointment is generally preferable. A reason is that an on-the-hoof approach requires more skill and experience of the pastor than a more structured situation. Effective pastoral care is difficult, so anything that can increase the chances of being more effective needs to be used. Moving the process from the distractions of the contact situation to the structure of a quiet office can help the pastor enormously.

Sometimes there may be a good reason for attempting to help someone without a separate appointment. The contact setting may be quiet and appropriate. For example, the contact may be in the form of a pastoral visit. The person may "drop by" the pastor's office and it might be more convenient for the pastor to see the person immediately than to send the person away to come back another time, or the problem may be genuinely urgent.

Whatever way the contact occurs, the first need is to ascertain the general nature of the request. This is particularly appropriate with a telephone call when someone asks for an appointment to see the pastor. The pastor's response needs to be something like, "Can you give me a general idea of what the appointment is for?" In this way the pastor checks to see if it is a personal request, and ascertains the general nature of the problem, such as marriage difficulty, failure of grades, or religious doubts. If a person unleashes an avalanche of detail after requesting an appointment, it is generally best to try to stem this off by saying, "Let's talk in more detail about this when you come for your appointment." Then the pastor should go ahead and set up an appointment. On the other hand, if the person has presented a problem on the phone without a request for an appointment, and starts giving a lot of confusing detail, the pastor should break in, indicating there is far too much material to digest over the phone in a few minutes, and suggest that the person make an appointment so she or he can take the time to listen to the details.

A suicide threat is a special contact situation where the goal is not to get an appointment made, but to get immediate help for the person. When a telephone call comes from a person indicating the problem is suicide, the first task of the pastor is to find out in what way she or he may be helpful. It needs to be recognized that most persons who really want to commit suicide will simply go ahead and kill themselves. Therefore, if a contact is made, there is a reason involved, generally that they want the pastor, in some way, to stop them. Therefore, as soon as possible, it should be determined why the person has called and what is expected.

If a person has already taken an overdose of pills, it generally means that the pastor should request an ambulance or a police unit to go to the person's house as soon as possible. At other times a person will call the pastor out of fear that she or he cannot contain suicidal impulses and, therefore, seeks protection as much as anything else. In special circumstances, it may be necessary for the pastor to heroically stay the night with the person to persuade her or him that life is worthwhile, but normally this is unnecessary because of hospital emergency rooms, and is recommended only as a course of action of last choice. If the person is a parishioner with great trust in the pastor, the pastor can try to persuade the person over the telephone to have a friend or neighbor take her or him to a nearby hospital, promising to meet them there. With a single, isolated parishioner whom the pastor knows, it may be necessary for the pastor to alert the hospital and then take the person to the hospital herself or himself. Again the pastor will be wise to use herself or himself only as a resource of last resort.

An important dimension in all of this is the relationship the pastor already has with the parishioner seeking help. One young pastor, awakened by a person he knew well who was "ending it all in a few minutes," had the presence of mind to ask her to put on a kettle of water because he would be right over to have a cup of tea. It worked! It got the person doing something for someone she liked as a way of saying she was still of worth. He was eventually able to get her to a hospital emergency room.

The importance of hospitalization for persons who contact the pastor because of potential suicide cannot be overstressed. The hospital is appropriate not only because it can provide a 24-hour watch on the person, but because of the biochemical studies of the last decades into the nature of primary affective disorders. (Greene et al 1976). Through changes in the biochemical systems (norepinephrine, seratonin, and dopamine levels in the brain stem) of persons with a primary affective disorder, many of these persons are driven by the resulting depression to suicidal thoughts and even attempts at suicide. Consequently, it becomes futile for pastors to seek external reasons for suicidal fear from such persons. In fact, questioning about suicide often makes such persons more desperate and hence, more likely to commit suicide. The sooner a person with a biochemical imbalance can be given medication under medical supervision, the sooner a recovery of biochemical homeostasis and the loss of suicidal impulses will take place.

As the suicide threat situations illustrate, if the pastor can't be of help to a person, the person should be referred immediately. It is the pastor's task to constantly assess, in the contact situation, the chances of helping the person and assess whether the person would be better served by referral. The sooner this determination can be made, the more effective the pastoral care. It is damaging for a person to have her or his hopes raised, experience the pastor as unhelpful, and then face a deeper form of despair and depression than before. Using up the small reservoir of hope can leave a person unmotivated to seek the more skilled specialists that are available.

Ineffective pastoral care, in many cases, actually has such an iatrogenic effect (treatment makes the person sicker) that later treatment has first to remedy the damage done by previous attempts to help. The contact is the first point where a referral decision needs to be made to minimize iatrogenic effects. Hence, it is important for the pastor to get from the person a general idea of the problem being presented, at the point of contact, as a way of estimating whether she or he can help. Admittedly, it may not be possible to make a referral decision quickly, at the point of contact, but in those cases where it is obvious that the problem is beyond the pastor's training, or for some other reason the pastor is not going to be able to help, she or he should attempt to refer without even trying to see the person. Of course, if the person refuses to be referred (and it is not a suicide situation), the pastor may then set up an appointment to seek the reasons for the resistance to the referral. But when this is done and the reason for the appointment is made clear to the person iatrogenic effects are minimized because hopes have not been falsely fostered.

There are many other problems associated with the contact. One of these involves a call from a third party, that is, a spouse or relative or friend of the one who is needing help. In such cases, the author thanks the person for calling and indicates whether he will be willing to see the person. If he is not willing, he tries to give the reason, such as other appointments, and suggests another resource. If he is willing to see the person, he indicates that he wants the third party to help by having the nominated client phone for an appointment. It is particularly important to rigidly adhere to this procedure when a parent has phoned to make an appointment for her or his teenager. The pastor will discover that most third parties are not malicious, interfering busybodies; they generally will quickly cooperate when the value of having the person they are concerned about make the appointment herself or himself is stressed.

Some third parties indicate they have suggested to the person needing help that she or he make an appointment to see the pastor but the person refuses. Rather than devising ways to manipulate the person into seeing the pastor, it is a simple matter to have the third party set up an appointment with the pastor herself or himself to discuss this problem. In this way the pastor sees if the third-party contact is an indirect way for that person to seek help for herself or himself. Sometimes the third-party call begins: "I've got a friend (whom the caller will not identify) . . ." which is really a way of seeking personal help for herself or himself. Such a person can be encouraged to seek an appointment to talk about the matter.

In one example of a difficult third-party situation, a pastor was approached by a wealthy but infrequent attending member of his church and asked to visit her daughter-in-law to tell her she needed to see a psychiatrist. Her son had been a wonderful person she said, until he had married the daughter-in-law from the "other side of the tracks." The woman felt the daughter-in-law had only married her son for the money. She was turning to the pastor because her husband had died two years before. Unfortunately, the pastor, after some hesitation, did eventually visit the daughter-in-law and got involved in a first-class mess. The fatal mistake was to assume the role of the woman agent whether he intended to be or not.

Manipulation attempts at the point of contact can be a problem. Manipulators, when they contact the pastor, are always trying to get her or him to do something. Some contact the pastor because they want to get money (often for alcohol or drugs) and will play the "help" game as long as it seems they have a "soft touch." Others come because they want the pastor to legitimatize something. For example, a woman, a total stranger, requested a pastor to write a job reference. When the pastor refused because he didn't know her, she started to cry over the phone and indicated how desperately she needed work. The pastor made an appointment, for a few hours later, to talk to her about the situation, without promising any reference. She was a nurse who had been fired from her previous three positions for stealing drugs. The pastor said he would support her job application if she was truthful about her record so that she would not have access to drugs. The woman was eventually hired on this basis and on the condition that she get outpatient psychiatric treatment. The chance for a new life came about because a pastor would not be manipulated, and turned the process into a caring transaction where the totality of the person's needs were considered. In this way very effective pastoral care was rendered.

One of the more difficult forms of manipulation is where a second person is brought to an appointment without notice. For example, a pastor was contacted about a "personal problem" by a woman who then appeared at the pastor's door with her husband. The pastor looked very surprised when this happened and indicated there must be some misunderstanding as he thought he was seeing only the person who phoned. Sometimes it will happen that the second person is simply acting as a chauffeur and will be happy to sit in the waiting area. Other times, raising the question of misunderstanding will produce an angry (guilty) defense as to why the other person should be present. In this situation the author generally indicates that he will see both as long as he is clear who is seeking help and why the other person's presence is necessary. Once this issue is dismissed at the beginning, a lot of things generally fall into place and the rest of the session is relatively easy.

When an unannounced conjoint situation occurs, it generally involves a marriage or girl friend/boy friend problem. This poses special difficulties for the author because his practice is not to see couples conjointly until after he has evaluated each one individually in one or two sessions each (Greene 1970, Moss and Lee 1975). In the case of a married couple, after ascertaining that the marriage and not the individual person is the problem, the author explains his marriage therapy procedures and suggests that the couple decide there and then who will remain for the rest of this session and then set up another appointment for the other person. The pastor should carefully note the interaction when the decision is being made in front of him. It is direct data on how decisions are probably made in the marriage.

A more common problem for the pastor at the point of contact is "panic merchants" (hysterics). Generally they are crying, upset, anxious and/or depressed and insist that something awful will happen if something is not done immediately. The message is to do something quickly because they can't stand it. There are, of course, many variations to this theme, including a hint or threat of suicide if the pastor does not seem to be jumping fast enough. The problem here is to accept the fact that such people are really experiencing inner pain and to communicate this acceptance, but not to rush and set up an immediate appointment. The author deliberately likes to schedule an appointment for the next morning if the call is at night, or in the afternoon if the call is in the morning. This tests the ability of the person to delay gratification of his or her wishes for at least a few hours. Technically stated, it tests a person's ego strength (inner positive resources). The author has never ceased to be amazed, if he displays empathy and sets up an appointment, how calm a lot of these people quickly become. They often testify that it greatly helped just to know they would be seeing the pastor soon and could depend on the appointment. It is not uncommon in some cases that the person feels the session is not needed before reaching the pastor's door. On the other hand, if when contacting the pastor the person thinks she or he "can't make it" (especially at night), the pastor needs to suggest that the problem is serious enough for the person to go to the emergency room of a hospital. This move deals with the underlying ambivalence and generally results in either the person deciding to wait until the appointment, or to actually go to the emergency room for psychiatric care. By making an appointment and not jumping to immediately gratify the person's needs, the pastor quickly ascertains those who are beyond his help at the contact stage.

A problem can emerge after an appointment has been made. The spouse sometimes phones the pastor and wants to talk about the person who has made the appointment in an effort to "assist" the pastor. In this case the pastor would do well to follow the example of Harry Stack Sullivan (1954) who says something to the effect: "What did you have in mind to talk about? Do *you* need a counselor?" Generally the spouse says, "No, it's my husband/wife." Then Sullivan says, "I should very much like to get all of the facts, but I would rather wait a little as I don't want to be unduly confused by too many facts all at once." As most persons have never thought of the possibility of confusing the therapist, such a statement is generally enough to satisfy the caller.

There is an infinite variety of ways contacts are made with a pastor or a pastoral therapist. Perhaps one of the most interesting of contacts is described by Robert Lindner (1955) in his case called, "Come Over Red Rover." As he describes the contact, he says, "We met, not across the desk, but over the heads of an audience at a meeting . . . Someone called, 'Are there any negroes on the list? I demand to know why negroes have been deliberately excluded from the panel'." Eventually, this person, who proved to be a left-wing political activist, phoned to make an appointment with Lindner and then went through a successful therapeutic experience with him.

Description

There is no correct way to describe a person. Yet there are some simple irreducible elements which are needed if the description is to be adequate. These are: age, occupation, height, weight, dress, face (especially eyes, nose, and mouth), voice, and gestures. The following are descriptions of four persons who presented themselves to a pastor for help. They have been selected because they clearly illustrate the value of an accurate description.

1. Ms. Anderson is a 28-year-old computer programmer. She is slim, 5'7" tall and weighs 115 lbs. She has blond hair neatly kept, blue eyes, and a sharply featured face. Her suit, made of an expensive dark brown cloth, did not have a crease out of place. Her light brown shoes were immaculately polished. She enhanced her tanned face (it was winter) with carefully applied makeup. Even though she spoke with a clear, command-ing voice, she had great difficulty looking at the counselor.

Comment: The perfectionism of this description suggests that Ms. Anderson may have some obsessive-compulsive qualities to her personality. Her suit does not have a crease out of place, her hair looks neat, and her shoes are immaculately polished. Other evidence comes from the avoiding look and the feeling that an obsessive-compulsive person would fit well into an occupation such as a computer program-mer. Slim persons (ectomorphs) are also often noted for being "worrywarts" (obsessive).

2. Mrs. Bartollo is a 32-year-old housewife with three children. She is 5'3" tall and seems to be 60 to 70 lb overweight. Her pink blouse clashed with her dark blue suit, which needed dry cleaning. Mrs. Bartollo's dark hair was disheveled and her lipstick, applied without concern for the natural contours of her lips, gave a grotesque appearance. Her brown eyes had a glazed, distant look to them, and seemed filled with a deep anger. She spoke with a flat monotonous tone.

Comment: The messy quality of her appearance points to depression. However, the glazed, distant look to eyes filled with deep anger, and the flattened affect, suggests a schizophrenic process. Both her messiness and overweight suggest that she is so focused on her internal world that she is not greatly concerned with how she looks to others.

3. Mr. Riley is a 35-year-old art teacher, married, and has two sons. He is 6' tall and weighs 180 lb. His "mod" clothes with large lapels and his long

hair gave him a striking appearance. He wore expensive Italian shoes and a handerchief in the upper left-hand pocket. When speaking he often rolled his eyes and grimaced. He spoke in an affected, plum-in-the-mouth manner.

Comment: The whole style of his dress is so distinctive that it draws a great deal of attention to him. He would stand out in a crowd. All of this suggests a narcissistic personality with some touches of hysteria and the possibility of some homosexual behavior.

4. Mr. Kapolka is a 5'0"-200 lb man, somewhere in his late 40s or early 50s. He wore a work shirt, overalls, and heavy, well-worn boots. He carried a "stocking hat" in his hand. His eyes tended to be downcast when he spoke, while his voice had a rapid whiney quality to it. A large round doleful face completed the picture.

Comment: He appears to be suffering from depression. Whether this is a reactive depression or a primary affective disorder would need to be discerned from the history of this man, including a family genetic history.

Initial Behavior

In recent years, the notion of body language has gained popular attention through the paperback market. Few students of human behavior dispute the fact that nonverbal communication (gesture, facial expression, and body posture) plays a major role in human transactions. Actors have used knowledge of body language for centuries with good effect. The more important question for the pastor is how far she or he can go in interpreting the behavioral communications received from persons who come seeking help, especially when a lot of the statements in popular literature have very little scientific support and seem to be more the figment of the writer's imagination than anything else.

While a pastor needs to be cautious about overinterpreting body language, there are gestures and facial expressions credited by some experimental support as being useful in evaluating persons. Why not use these, at least, especially as the person is generally unconscious of the gesture. Further, even though many of the gestures and facial expressions may not always have the same meaning, they can form useful auxiliary data when interpreted in conjunction with all of the other material of the presenting transference. Such behavioral data helps form the important gestalt with which the person presents herself or himself to the pastor, and by looking for this behavior and data from other sources, wild evaluations can be avoided.

One excellent scientific article on the subject of human gestures and facial expressions was written by Christopher Brannigan and David Humphries (1969). They reported conclusions based on observations of children between the ages of three and five. Such children are less inhibited and tend to communicate with verbal symbols less than adults. According to Brannigan and Humphries, facial expressions arise mainly from two areas, the eyes and the mouth. When a child changes the line of the mouth, she or he indicates a mood change. If this line curves up, she or he is happy but if the line curves down, she or he is sad. When the child raises her or his eyebrows, she or he is pleasantly surprised, and this raising movement is generally accompanied by a broad smile. The line of the mouth has been used by clinicians for a long time, but the experimental confirmation suggests that other practices handed down by clinicians may be used with some confidence. Using the raised eyebrow as an indication also makes sense. However, films of adults have shown that eyebrow raising, which sometimes suddenly appears in a person about to smile, suggests that the preceding remarks or events are of special interest to the person, rather than a pleasant surprise.

By watching conflict between children, the researchers were able to distinguish between an offensive and defensive beating posture. The offensive beating posture is where the child develops an angry frown, thrusts her or his tense lips and chin forward and raises the arms as if to strike a blow, called a beat, with the palm of the hands facing the opponent. In a defensive beating posture the other child crouches, cries, or runs away after raising an arm as if to ward off the blow. Generally the whole face flushes to signal an actual or possible defeat. In adults, these behaviorial gestures are generally disguised. In the offensive situation, the adult will touch the chin or cheek with thumb and forefinger and with the palm facing the other person (opponent). In the defensive form, the hand moves back as if to beat in return, but the gesture is modified by palm being placed on the back of the neck. In a woman this defensive gesture can be turned into a sophisticated grooming action. Another example is the driver who makes a mistake that could have been costly who does a quick grooming movement through her or his hair followed by a hand-to-neck posture.

W. John Smith (1973) did a study on the significance of tongue showing.

In the child, the showing of the tongue was seen as defiance or mockery. However, after watching films of primates, school children, adults, and older people, Smith came to the conclusion that tongue showing indicated a reluctance of the person, for whatever the reason, to engage in social intercourse. This interpretation seems understandable, recalling that when one gets preoccupied in a task, one often unknowingly sticks out the tongue until someone points this out.

Studies such as these should alert the pastor to the value of observing gestures, facial expressions, and body movements when interviewing and particularly when trying to give effective pastoral care or in evaluating persons for pastoral therapy. But because the initial few moments of an interview, especially the first, involved heightened anxiety, the initial behavior is of special significance. The following correlations of gestures with problem areas of clients has not been experimentally validated, but comes from the practice of pastoral therapists where other data tended to confirm the interpretations given. For example, a man who was a stranger to a pastor and not a member of his church came to see him after setting up an appointment for "help with a marriage problem." The man carried his jacket over his arm as he entered the pastor's office, placed it over his lap when he sat down, and then started to twist it quite vigorously. The first thing the pastor thought this indicated was that the person was anxious and the jacket acted as a comforting "Linus blanket." It seemed to indicate that he wouldn't stay long because he was ready, jacket in lap, to make a quick exit. Another thought was that he was symbolically saying he was so angry at his wife he would like to wring her neck. Data from other sources suggested that both interpretations could be correct. However, as he did not return for a second appointment, no other material became available to confirm or deny these interpretations.

In another situation, a young woman came into the office for the first interview, sat down in her overcoat with her arms out of the sleeves, and proceeded to nestle into the coat, wrapping it around herself. The room was at comfortable temperature. The pastor wondered if the coat wrapping was a defensive gesture, but other material pointed to considerable deprivation, so the pastor came to see it as a symbolic wish to be hugged. When he verbalized this in a later session, the woman was able to share her extreme loneliness and get to the core of her personality dynamics.

There are many other initial behaviors which could be discussed. Arm or leg crossing can occur when a person feels challenged or threatened. A hand over a mouth may indicate the person is trying not to incriminate himself or herself. When a person looks at the pastor, then drops the eyes or looks aside it is generally an attempt to hide something of which she or he is ashamed. A classic situation is where a person says no to a question but slightly nods the head, which means yes. A person consistantly slipping a shoe on or off indicates she or he is conflicted about something. Slipping a ring on and off the finger could indicate the person's ambivalence about continuing in a marriage. And clasping hands in a prayer-like gesture can mean the person is trying to justify what she or he is saying to herself or himself.

Nail biting has received attention from behavioral sciences over the years, and it has been interpreted generally as indicating anxiety, but evidence is now coming forward that nail biters are anxious because they are uncertain about their own identities. In men nail biting seems to indicate particularly their fear of being emasculated. The scratching or rubbing of a nose is associated with aggression. People who scratch or rub the nose generally are passive-aggressives who turn their anger upon themselves. Too much touching and stroking of the hair is considered narcissistic, while slow, rotating ankle movement may be indicative of a sensuous person. Persons who frequently take off their glasses could use denial heavily as a defense, and those who make sudden gestures, such as sharp stabbing with a finger or pounding with the fist, tend to be an impulsive.

The following write-up and discussion is intended to underscore the importance of initial behavior for the pastor and to encourage its recording for supervisory purposes.

Write-up No. 2

Identifying Information

Session: No. 1
Date: May 4, 1979
Place: First Methodist Church, Townsville, Tasmania
Client: Mrs. Hill
 463 Garrett Place
 Townsville, Tasmania
 Phone: GB 2-1201
Pastor: A. Hanford

Contact: Mrs. Hill phoned and made an appointment because of "marriage difficulties." She was a member of the church but because she was not regular in attendance, was only slightly known to the pastor.

Description: Mrs. Hill is a 30-year-old married woman with two small children. She is 5'7" tall and weighs 125 lb. To the pastor she appeared strikingly beautiful. She has blond hair and blue eyes, was attractively dressed in an expensive outfit with matching blue jacket and pants, and her makeup was done carefully.

Initial Behavior: Next to the pastor's office in the church was a large social room where, by custom, coffee was generally available. When Mrs. Hill entered the office, she was carrying two cups of coffee.

When the pastor brought this write-up into supervision, the issue which clearly emerged was whether the woman wanted a social relationship or a helping one. In bringing in the two cups of coffee, she was, in effect, saying she didn't know yet whether she was ready to face the pain of the reality of her marriage. In the next interview, when she again brought in coffee, the pastor gently asked if she was unconsciously communicating anything by this. The woman reflected awhile and then was able to discuss her ambivalence about being helped. This note of honesty place the relationship on a new basis and enabled some effective pastoral care to take place, all because the pastor raised the issue of the initial behavior with the person.

Initial Words
The initial words of an interview are often an important clue to the deeper thought and feelings of a person seeking help from a pastor. For example, a person who had seen a pastor (who was under supervision) for about 20 sessions returned after a three-week Christmas break mutually agreed upon. Her first words were, "It's been a long time!" Material from the rest of that particular session suggested that the person found the sessions with the pastor extremely valuable and had developed a useful form of dependency on him as a result.

One of the most important initial sentences in therapy is "How are you?" Sometimes this can be a form of social pleasantness, but generally it carries a deeper meaning, especially if it tends to occur in the initial few moments after a few sessions have gone by. Often it can indicate the formation of a working alliance in pastoral therapy, but also it can indicate the person can't admit the importance of the dependency that goes with that alliance. It is saying something to the effect that the person can't admit the intensity of her or his needs, that the person considers the pastor to be of life-and-death importance, or that the person has a desperate need to see the pastor in an ideal way.

If the initial words are important for long-term pastoral psychotherapy, they are equally valuable for short-term pastoral care. The following write-up of a first session illustrates this.

Write-up No. 3

Identifying Information

    Session: No. 1

    Date: July 23, 1981

    Place: Evangelical Church, St. Charles, Alaska

    Client: Mr. Evers

            12 Western Street, St. Charles, Alaska

            Phone: Home—DA 8-2212

                    Work—WE 6-5928

    Associate Pastor: Joe Smith

Contact: The person phoned and asked for an appointment for himself. He was not a member of the church but had heard of the pastor from a friend. He was having difficulties with a supervisor at his place of employment.

Description: The client is 6'2" tall, weighs 200 lb, and has ink black hair and brown eyes. He was dressed in a brown sports jacket, dark brown pants, orange shirt, and brown shoes—all looked good together.

Initial Behavior: Mr. Evers offered his hand and grinned. He was smoking a curved pipe. He sat in the chair that the pastor offered while the pastor closed the door of his study. Mr. Evers, looking nervous, fidgeted with his pipe.

Initial Words: After a long pause, he finally said, "I suppose you want to know something about me (if that is where you want to start). I came into this world with a bang! My pregnant mother was visiting my father on board this battleship in Norfolk harbor. Being wartime, the gun was loaded and my brother pulled the cord and the gun went off with a bang. My father has been slightly deaf since then. My mother dropped me on the spot. I am the only child born with a one-gun salute."

The key words are: "I came into the world with a bang!" The fact seems to be that his mother gave birth to him while on a visit to his father at Norfolk Naval Base, and a gun explosion may have made his mother nervous and hastened his birth. Assuming the basic facts are accurate it is obvious that this person likes to present himself in as dramatic and embellished a fashion as possible. This could indicate some narcissism, but it also points to his need to be interesting and his fear of being looked upon as "dullsville," as he later called it. Moreover, the phrase implies this man constantly packages himself in a way that he thinks will "sell" to the person with whom he is interacting. The "bang" motif also suggests that he is full of rage which needs to come out, but which he fears will come out in a destructive explosion. While the initial words suggest some hysterical as well as some narcissistic dynamics, the underlying feeling is that this man is more sociopathic than anything else and is used to manipulating the facts whenever it suits his purpose. Later material supported this evaluation.

Presenting Complaint or Problem

The presenting complaint is really the problem as the one seeking help sees it. Generally, it reflects the way the internal psychic pain shows itself, but sometimes the pain seems so acute that it shows up in not one, but many complaints. The chief of these needs to be recorded as a source of data for determination of presenting transference.

The chief complaint can cover an enormous range of problems. Some examples of these follow.

1. "I procrastinate."
2. "My wife refuses to have sex with me."
3. "I have stopped believing in the Bible."
4. "I constantly need to check my front door to see that it is locked."
5. "I've been working all of these years. I don't get anywhere."
6. "My wife and I can't communicate."
7. "I've been lost since my father died."
8. "I'm bored now that my children are in school."
9. "I never knew I was adopted! I must find out more."
10. "My husband is having an affair."
11. "My children are driving me crazy."

12. "I feel hopeless and lost. Life no longer has any meaning."
13. "I don't know whether to go back to my husband, or divorce him and marry my boy friend."

Sometimes these complaints may not be very useful for an evaluation, but they round out the picture and offer yet another source of how the person presents herself or himself in the first few moments of the interview. It is particularly useful in evaluating the pragmatic person who sees life in terms of problems more than anything else. The task of the pastor in pastoral care or pastoral therapy is to shift the focus of the person seeking help from her or his problems to the dynamics that exist behind the symptoms and problems.

At this stage, it seems pertinent to point out that person-centered pastoral care and pastoral therapy are entirely different from the problem-centered approach as is practiced by many pastors. The reason for this is that problems, complaints, or symptoms tend to deal with a surface level of the personality, as is recognized by healing-helping professionals. Jack Douglas (1970), a sociologist who studied suicide centers, discovered that advertising suicide prevention may actually cause more people to think of ordinary problems in suicidal terms. He found that most people who call suicide prevention centers aren't thinking of killing themselves, they just want to talk about their problems and do it in terms of suicide because they think that is what the center is for.

Douglas' work clearly refers to the packaging phenomenon familiar to those who work in a clinic for some special kind of problem. For example, the author once worked in an alcoholism clinic, which, because it was a better treatment facility and program than was being offered for other problems, would attract drug addicts and mentally ill persons, all claiming they were alcoholics. Similarly, the pastor needs to be aware that persons who are emotionally in pain will sometimes package their personal hurts as a problem with prayer, or as a problem with a biblical passage or a theological doctrine.

The reverse side of the packaging problem is that it may lead a person to seek out a specific helping professional. The paranoid person will be seen in greater proportions by lawyers because she or he frequently resorts to litigation as a means of solving problems. On the other hand, the hypochrondriac is more likely to approach a general practitioner of medicine than anyone else because, when under pressure and anxious, her or his anxiety will come out in the form of vague physiological symptoms. The manic may get politically active and consult a precinct captain. The obsessive-compulsive may turn to the ritual of religion and go to a pastor for help. At the same time, the dependent person may go to a local bar, and so on. Because of the tendency for many to package problems there will always be a need for persons in occupations like teaching, ministry, bar-tending, and hairdressing to act as "gatekeepers" for the more specialized and highly trained therapeutic professionals.

The presenting complaint is generally the launching pad into the main content of the first interview and it often calls for a response by the pastor. Sometimes the presenting problem is not clear. It would be wise for the pastor to ask what the person means when the words used are not clear. If this is done in an inquiring rather than a critical spirit, the person seeking help will sense through the question or two that the pastor is really interested in him or her. Again, if the presenting problem is too vague, the pastor can ask the person if she or he could be a little more specific. On the other hand, if the presenting problem is clear, the pastor may need to ask for an example or two as a means of checking to see if the person is exaggerating. In general, the presenting symptom gives the pastor a chance to start acting as a facilitator of the process whereby the person reveals what she or he can of herself or himself.

The following write-up of a case begins with the initial phase of the first interview and continues through the presenting problem. In this case it becomes clear that the presenting problem is a crucial feature of the presentation.

Write-up No. 4

Identifying Information

Session: No. 1
Date: February 6, 1981
Place: Christ Episcopal Church, Chelsea, Texas
Client: Mr. J. Brown
12 Grove Street, Chelsea, Texas
Phone: GR 6-4262
Assistant Pastor: Jack Davis

Contact: The pastor met Mr. Brown after worship during the summer vacation. Mr. Brown wanted to talk to him immediately.

Description: Mr. Brown, a 17-year-old senior in high school, is 6'1" tall and weighs 200 lbs. He has an athletic build, but his neat gray suit disguised this somewhat. He has dark, bushy hair, a broad face which displayed a "shadow beard," brown eyes, and long sideburns. When he spoke, it was in a slightly pitched, nervous voice.

Initial Behavior: Mr. Brown sat on the first available chair, but after the pastor sat in the chair behind his desk, he moved to a chair closer to the desk. He began to wring his hands and run them over his face in jerky movements.

Initial Words: "I'm in some real trouble." He then went on to say, "I did something real bad a couple of days ago and I thought you could help me, being a minister and all."

Presenting Complaint or Problem: He said he had molested a little girl two days ago and was either going to be arrested and be put in jail, or else sent to a mental hospital.

To summarize, contact, description, initial behavior, initial words and presenting problems are all elements of the way a person presents herself or himself in the first moments of the initial session. Referred to as the presenting relationship, it also has been called by the Latin term prima vista diagnose. *It is the total way a person presents herself or himself and not just the problem that is presented.* Of course, the presenting takes place throughout the whole of the session, but it generally is clearest in the first few moments before the pastor is swamped by the material that follows. Two or three minutes of alert attention at this stage can be worth pages of detailed history later on.

With this chapter's stress on looking for the presenting transference for evaluation purposes, the question of diagnostic syndromes gets raised. The reader is referred to a textbook by Roger MacKinnon and Robert Michels (1971) for a general study of this matter. The presenting diagnosis, however, has not gained enough exactness for any one set of presenting behaviors to represent any one syndrome. Rather, each presenting relationship will need to be seen for the way it points to a general diagnosis and the unique way it portrays each person's life.

Hopefully, however, enough has been said for the pastor wanting to become more effective in pastoral care and/or pastoral therapy to encourage her or him to observe presenting behavior and record these observations for supervision, discussion, and learning.

2 : Initial Interview

Evidence for the presenting transference continues after the first few moments of the initial interview. Yet because the pastor is generally busy absorbing the content of the session or interacting with the person seeking help, it becomes difficult to keep the idea of the presenting transference as a focus. Soon the pastor becomes involved in a complex process.

Often the person seeking help will be anxious and talk incessantly, filling in the time with words. Whether the talking is beneficial for the person or not, it enables the pastor to adopt a passive role and appear to be confident about pastoral care or pastoral therapy. The pastor can then justify her or his passivity as good listening or can rationalize this by saying that talking is good for the person (catharsis). If the client doesn't talk, the pastor can remain silent in the hope that the resulting anxiety will "encourage" the person to talk. Sometimes this manipulation succeeds, yet at other times it results in a silent power struggle. Generally, it leads the person to break off the relationship.

When the person doesn't talk and the pastor wants to avoid a silence, he can resort to asking questions. Just like the person's need to talk, and silences, a question is a legitimate part of pastoral care and pastoral therapy, but like them, when overused as a crutch for the pastor or person to avoid anxiety, it can block effective communication. This is because too many questions can reinforce or foster dependency on the questioner. Such questioning means that the pastor, who asks questions, controls the content of the session, and presupposes that the pastor knows the right questions to ask in the first place.

To illustrate why we should use questions sparingly, let's envisage the scene where the owner of a house has died, and a visitor comes to the door and asks if the owner is in. How does one answer? Obviously, the question is out of its appropriate context; it just doesn't fit the situation anymore. A statement of the death of the owner is made to the caller and the explanation shifts the frame of reference. Questions always run the risk of being off base or out of the right frame of reference. In fact, questions can become annoying or even provocative, thus thwarting the development of a working alliance, which is discussed in chapter 5.

In an interview the pastor should act in a variety of ways, sometimes being passive, sometimes allowing silences, and sometimes asking questions, and in doing so not resort to the overuse of any one method. Even so, for effective pastoral care or pastoral therapy, the focus of the pastor needs to be more on the processes in the person seeking help than on what the pastor does. It is better to assume that the person seeking help will usually talk. When the person is unable to do this, the pastor's curiosity needs to be raised rather than her or his panic button pressed. The pastor can assume that the person who has taken the trouble to phone, make an appointment, and then come to see her or him, is seeking something. If the person then doesn't talk, or is confused, it generally is not willful, perverse behavior, but simply a means of communicating the existence of resistances for which she or he needs the help of the pastor. The pastor's attention, therefore, needs to be on potential resistances that might be blocking the natural flow of the interview.

There are some blocks that frequently occur in the first session. Sometimes the person needs to talk about the matter of confidentiality before she or he is willing to share any significant material. This is an issue about which the pastor needs to be particularly sensitive as a possible source of resistance, because the degree of professionalism and discreetness varies enormously among ministers, and because church communities can be vicious rumor mills. For this reason the person coming for help from a pastor will often need extra assurance about confidentiality.

Another reason for the person resisting sharing her or his deeper self can be a sense of shame for even needing to seek personal help. Unfortunately, such persons feel that in order to be Christians they have to be perfect; hence seeking help is seen as having failed to be a Christian (perfect). Before such a person will be ready to share, reassurance is needed from the pastor that her or his acceptance as a person is based upon grace and not works. In dealing with the help-seeking person to revealing herself or himself, the pastor is able to be "the Gospel" to the person at the moment.

A fear with which it is a little more difficult to deal, but which often results in resistance to the development of any significant relationship with the pastor, is the fear of dependency. The person does not fear the dependency as such, but the fantasy about what will happen once the dependency develops. Once the person becomes dependent, will the pastor be able to meet her or his dependency needs, such as being available if she or he is hurting in any way? Or will the pastor take advantage of her or him once she or he is dependent and hence in the pastor's power? While fantasies associated with dependency rarely emerge in an initial interview, they nevertheless can operate at a deep level; it is still possible for the pastor to give assurances by saying that a little dependency is normal in any helpful relationship. By being honest and open about dependency, and by showing the person that she or he, the pastor, will not try to foster any more than is necessary, the resistance to dependency generally can be overcome.

Resistances can also be fostered by the introduction of mechanized recording devices. A tape recorder with a reel rotating in front of the person's eyes can be very distracting, to say the least. The cassette type of recorder has lessened this distracting quality but taping of any kind, audio or video, can interfere in the development of a response necessary for any significant sharing. In any case, no taping should take place without the written consent of the person, but even where the pastor goes to the trouble of having the person sign such a consent form a feeling of intrusion can occur, and resistance to sharing fostered.

The author remembers well a situation where he was requested to make available to the group supervision class of the institution where he was in training, a video tape of an interview. A rather quiet, interesting woman whom the author had seen twice, and with whom he seemed to have a good rapport, was chosen for the taping interview. But the request meant changing the next session to a special video-taping room, and, even though the author had gained the person's permission to do the taping, and had spent half an hour the previous session having the person focus on her feelings about being taped, the taping session was an outright disaster.

The young woman spent most of the session saying how angry she was in a multitude of ways. She was late for the session, she was silent for long stretches, and was ready to disagree at the slightest hint of any interpretation. When the author tried to focus on her anger, she angrily denied she was angry and insisted that the taping made no difference.

Knowledge of the intrusive effect of taping also comes out of the author's experience of four years on a regional membership committee of the American Association of Pastoral Counselors. In the regional committee, audio tapes were required from the applicants for membership and it was obvious that where the pastor introduced the taping as a last minute matter because it was required for her or his examination, the person was generally angry and the session not typical. In noting that taping can more easily produce resistance than seems to have been acknowledged in pastoral therapy in the past, it is not being advocated that taping be dropped. However, taping ought not to be introduced until it has been thoroughly discussed with the person, and her or his feelings considered. Taping can be a particularly difficult problem with someone who has a paranoid type of personality.

The question of a person communicating something of her or his inner self is intimately linked with anxiety. If there is any one area that ought to receive the attention of the pastor during the first session of any pastoral care or therapy, it is the anxiety level of the person seeking help. Generally speaking, the higher the anxiety level, the higher the resistance and the more difficult it is to establish a working relationship. On the other hand, when a person doesn't have a great deal of anxiety, she or he may also resist revealing herself or himself because of not being sufficiently motivated to seek help. There is real truth in the quotation, placed on a church notice board, "Worry is like sand in an oyster; a little produces a pearl, too much kills the animal."

What is being proposed here is a model of pastoral care and pastoral therapy that accepts the notion that some anxiety is normal, and certainly necessary if effective pastoral care or pastoral therapy is to take place. It is also recognized that this idea is contrary to the popular view where the pastor is called in to calm someone when that person is perceived by a relative, friend, or another professional to be upset. Often implicit in such a request is the view that all anxiety is bad. Frankly, the evidence is that anxiety, if kept within the lower-to-medium range, can be an asset because it provides the energy for a person to work on herself or himself.

In cases where a person is hysterical, the pastor needs to help the person calm down and get her or his anxiety under some degree of control. With such a situation, the first task is to neutralize the excessive anxiety. The general rule, however, is to try to understand, not placate. Where placation and comforting take place in situations of extreme anxiety, they are only meant as a prelude to understanding and are only justified when the person is too anxious and distracted to be able to communicate coherently. Detailed examination of case write-ups of pastoral care situations indicate that in far too many situations the pastor attempts to counsel or placate when the person is not excessively anxious. As many of these write-ups came from ministers with enough self-esteem to allow their work to be examined, it can only be concluded that the need to placate, possibly because the anxiety of the person made the pastor feel uncomfortable, is a serious problem in ministry, undermining the effectiveness of much pastoral care. As an example, in one suburban church the associate minister had visited a woman parishioner in hospital, talking with her about her forthcoming hysterectomy, having her share her feelings and fears, and in general, preparing her for the operation. She was at peace. The night before the operation a shaken senior pastor who had been phoned by an anxious husband, insisted that the associate get out of bed and give the woman the sacraments, despite the fact that the woman and the associate had talked about the idea and rejected it. Needless to say, the sacraments idea was that of the husband, a wealthy parishioner. Sacraments had not been requested by the wife nor had the husband discussed them with her. Despite the protest of the associate, the senior minister insisted on his order being carried out as a means of placating the woman' husband, whose underlying needs he ignored.

For those pastors conducting the initial session of what promises to be pastoral therapy, the permitting of some degree of anxiety can speed up the evaluation process. In talking, slightly anxious persons are likely to reveal significant material more quickly. For as Anna Freud (1966) indicates, some anxiety is valuable because it "magnifies the diagnosis." Thus, it is that a competent pastoral therapist will learn to unconsciously monitor the anxiety level of a client in each session. Asking questions, pointing out puzzling inconsistencies, and showing genuine concern for self-destructive behavior are all ways for the pastoral therapist to raise sufficient anxiety to motivate a person to work on herself or himself. At the same time, toward the end of a session, the effective therapist tries to respond in ways that leave the client feeling good about the work done, the insights gained, and the fact that the anxiety at the beginning of the session has been brought under control.

The author has found so much resistance in students and ministers to the potentially constructive role of anxiety in a helping relationship, it is pertinent to add that the evidence for this is broader than just clinical. There is corroborative support from such diverse and independent fields as learning (Denenberg and Karas 1962), communication (Horland et al 1953) surgery (Florell 1971), and imprinting (Hess 1958). Research in these areas, while not always consistent, nevertheless supports the notion that some anxiety can be used constructively in a relationship to help persons change and adapt. The pastors and pastoral therapists need to monitor their clients' anxiety and be in touch with and in control of their own.

The following write-up illustrates a situation where the anxiety of a person required attention in the early part of the first interview.

Write-up No. 6
Identifying Information
    Session: No. 1

    Date: September 26, 1943

    Place: First Methodist Church, Tornado, Kansas

    Client: Mrs. Bloomfield
           25 Sever Street
           Tornado, Kansas
           Phone: Home—254-3681
                      Work—254-2400 Ext. 26

    Pastor: Sam Brown

Contact: Mrs. Bloomfield, a member and regular attendant at the church, and well-known to the pastor, telephoned for an appointment. She wanted to discuss her 12-year-old daughter with the pastor.

Description: Mrs. Bloomfield is a nervous woman in her late 30s. About 5'2" tall and weighing 130 lb, she wore comfortable clothes consisting of a brown, knee-length skirt, a matching sweater, and sturdy brown shoes. She had a bright, shining face, a pleasant if nervous smile, a mouthline which tended to curve down, fair hair and light blue eyes. Her voice was pitched nervously high.

Initial Behavior: Mrs. Bloomfield was on time for the appointment, but hesitated as she entered the room. She sat down in the offered chair in such a way as to only sit on the front edge.

Initial Words: "I don't want to waste your time, but I need to talk with someone who won't think I am silly."

Presenting Complaint or Problem: Mrs. Bloomfield indicated that a crisis had occured in her home because her husband was insisting that their severely mentally retarded daughter be placed in an institution. She was resisting this.

Main Summary of Material: For about 10 minutes Mrs. Bloomfield spoke quickly and in detail about the struggles of the family to cope with the mentally retarded daughter. She mentioned how draining the care of the child had been on everyone in the family, but felt that she could not bear the thought of the daughter now being institutionalized. At this point the pastor decided to try to deal with Mrs. Bloomfield's obvious anxiety and suggested that he give her "a breather" (she was almost breathless by this time) by stating what he understood she had said. At this, Mrs. Bloomfield smiled, nodded her head appreciably, and then slid back into the chair, at the same time giving a deep sigh of relief.

In this interview the pastor read the various ways Mrs. Bloomfield communicated that she was extremely nervous. The way she sat on the edge of the chair particularly suggested that she was prepared to take flight from the slightest thing, so he determined to take some of the pressure off her as soon as possible (he explained in supervision). He did this by the simple method of giving some feedback. Judging from her behaviorial responses he succeeded in lowering her anxiety enough for her to remain for the rest of the session.

In the following case the pastor was able to deal with his client's anxiety by discussing it with her.

Write-up No. 7
Identifying Information
Session: No. 1
Date: September 1, 1972

Place: Calvary Baptist Church, Dellas, Virginia
Client: Mrs. Hood
    2 Asbury Street
    Dellas, Virginia
    Phone: Home—DA8-6464
           Work—DA8-2000
Pastor: James Cook

Contact: Mrs. Hood phoned for an appointment and indicated that while she was not a member she had been referred by a work friend, Mrs. Green, who was a faithful and well-known member of the pastor's church.

Description: Mrs. Hood is a 26-year-old divorcee with a daughter five years of age. She is 5'5" tall and weighs 150 lb. Dressed in clean but slightly drab work clothes, she wore her light brown hair pulled back tight in a small ponytail. Her face appeared white and tense, her brown eyes had rings under them, and the line of her mouth slanted down despite her contant attempts to smile. Her voice was quick, loud, and sharp.

Initial Behavior: Mrs. Hood responded to the invitation to sit on the chair and immediately lit a cigarette after sitting down.

Initial Words: "Where do you want me to begin?" (The pastor then asked what the problem was.)

Presenting Complaint or Problem: "I am too dependent!" The pastor asked what she meant by "dependent" and asked if she would give him an example of her dependency problem. At this point Mrs. Hood gave a nervous laugh and crossed her legs. She then blurted out that she would try but was "awfully nervous." Because Mrs. Hood was able to verbalize her anxiety the pastor decided to focus on it. He assured her that anxiety is natural enough in anyone seeking help. Mrs. Hood replied, "But I think I am more anxious than most." "Tell me about that," the pastor said.

This exchange led Mrs. Hood and the pastor to explore many situations where she had been anxious in the past. During this discussion Mrs. Hood revealed that she had been in intense psychotherapy on twice-a-week basis with a psychiatrist, but had broken off the relationship eight months previously because she was becoming too anxious. The psychiatrist had interpreted to her that she was falling in love with him. By then the session had gone half an hour and the pastor, who was not trained to do intensive psychotherapy, felt it urgent to clarify if she was expecting psychotherapy from him. When asked, she said that she was hoping that he could do something for her because she couldn't afford the $50-per-session fees of the psychiatrist. The pastor indicated that he was not trained to do long-term intensive psychotherapy, and therefore would not attempt any treatment. However, he would be willing to work with her for a few sessions further to look at the reasons why she pulled out of therapy and if necessary, help her back into therapy with a competent therapist.

With some persons it may be appropriate to raise their anxiety level. Write-up No. 3, given earlier, is an example of such a situation involving a person with authority problems and a possible sociopathic personality. In this case the pastor, Pastor Smith, was a Ph.D. pastoral therapist specialist with Diplomate status in the American Association of Pastoral Counselors. For a large part of the initial interview the client, Mr. Evers, complained about his work supervisor not understanding him. All the examples he gave, however, suggested to the pastor that Mr. Evers didn't like to work within reasonable limits. So about two-thirds of the way through the first session the pastor deliberately raised the matter of a fee. Mr. Evers and his wife were both earning salaries that put them in the combined income bracket of $30,000. The pastor explained the policy of the church in offering therapeutic help to nonmembers for payment and that the payment was on a sliding scale according to the capacity of the people to pay. For this first session there would be no charge, but for later sessions there would be a fee of $20.00 a session. Mr. Evers became a little upset claiming that this was not reasonable and tried to give as many reasons as possible why he should not be charged anything. For the first time during the interview the pastor felt that Mr. Evers was no longer acting for the gallery and that they were really engaged in a meaningful relationship. As the time had run out, the pastor suggested that Mr. Evers think about the matter of the fee and come back the following week to discuss it further. There was little doubt in his mind that Mr. Evers' anger as well as anxiety had been raised and that he would have to determine if he was really motivated for change.

The words of Sullivan (1954) summarize well the position taken on anxiety in the preceding text.

"Anyone who proceeds without consideration for the disjunctive power of anxiety in human relationships will never learn interviewing. When there is no regard for anxiety, a true interview situation does not exist, instead, there may be just a person (the patient) trying to defend himself frantically from some kind of devil (the therapist) who seems determined to prove that the person is a double-dyed blankety-blank. This can be a spectacular human performance, but it does not yield psychiatric data relevant to therapeutic progress."

While Sullivan's words were addressed to psychiatrists, they apply equally well to pastors doing pastoral care or pastoral therapy.

Beyond indicating that resistances and the anxiety behind these resistances need to be a major concern of the pastor in any initial interview, it is very difficult to predict what the course of the initial interview will be. The pastor will learn how to follow the process of the interview through competent supervision. Hence, the pastor needs to carefully write up the main issues which emerge, and in the order with which they occur, so they can be discussed in the supervision.

As in write-up no. 7, if the pastor is convinced that a person needs a referral, she or he should start to work on this referral as soon as possible. If, for example, the person shows gross pathology it is better for the pastor not to stress this grossness but simply indicate that she or he does not have the training to deal with the specific problem the person brings. Then, any resistance to the referral can be dealt with as the proper focus of the pastoral care. Chapter 8 will look at the question of referral in detail. It is enough to note here that the end of the initial interview is another critical time when decisions regarding referral often need to be made. Again, if there is resistance to being referred, the pastor should not hesitate to make another appointment for the purpose of discussing the referral.

Assuming that the session has gone for approximately 40 minutes and the pastor sees that further interviews may be needed, she or he should spend the remaining time, presumably five minutes, to contract with the person for further sessions. This is generally effected by suggesting that the time is about to run out and that the person may want to talk further with the pastor. If the person agrees, the pastor then sets up another date and time. Following the practice of Richard Chessick, (1974) the author gives the person a card with the time and date on it. In any mixup about appointments the card can help clarify the matter immediately.

At the end of the initial interview the point is also reached where the difference in approach between pastoral care and pastoral therapy may affect the next decision made. If the pastor is trained in pastoral therapy or is being supervised by a trained therapist and wishes to explore the possibility of pastoral therapy with the person, she or he may continue for the next two or three sessions conducting a further evaluation of the person, including taking a personal history and giving tests, or having testing done by a qualified psychologist. On the other hand, without taking a formal history or employing testing, the pastor can continue to see the person on a pastoral care basis. Where this is done the pastor needs to keep active and make sure that the sessions have some concrete focus as a means of diminishing the emergence of transference, which is discussed further in chapter 6. Of course, even where a pastor is not trained in therapy and is not under supervision it would enhance his pastoral care if she or he had some history material and used both the history and the write-up of the initial interview for consultation purposes.

It also must be acknowledged that there are pastoral specialists who do not take a formal history and/or employ testing, who function as effective pastoral therapists because of skills at diagnosing from the presenting material and because of their training and qualifications. There are also some pastors who claim they are therapists and yet disavow any need for evaluation whatsoever, but this is a position recommended in this book. Very few pastors can just "fly by the seat of their pants" and do long-term work without developing serious misalliances (Langs 1976). This book stresses the need for a diagnosis, with a history and testing as valuable adjuncts to the presenting transference in developing that diagnosis. Furthermore, in offering two or three more sessions for the purpose of evaluation, the pastor is lessening pressure for an immediate magical cure. In fact, in suggesting the evaluation, the pastor will sometimes force into the open such magical expectations.

Sooner or later, the first session ends. There is no infallible rule as to what the length of a session should be, but whatever the normal length of time the pastor gives to seeing a person, whether it is 30, 40, or 50 minutes, she or he should be firm about not going beyond it this first session. The session's end is normally signaled by a cue, such as the statement, "Our time is up," which has to be said simply, without implying anything else.

Once in a while, the person tries to delay the termination of the session by trying to introduce new material. This is generally handled by saying, "Let's deal with that next time." However, if the person is persistent, the pastor may have to introduce a note of reality, such as, "I am sorry, I have another appointment, so we must stop now." If this does not work, the pastor needs to stand up or give some other behavorial cue as a way of indicating the interview is over. Generally, the tendency for the person to cling to the session is a diagnostic clue that she or he has considerable dependency which she or he is prepared to act-out (strictly speaking, act in). As discussed further in chapters 4, 5 and 6, acting out or in is where a person expresses an unconscious thought or feeling through action as a way of preventing the thought from becoming conscious.

Sometimes the person will indicate to the pastor that she or he hopes the pastor has a good week, or a good something while going out the door. This generally does not call for a response by the pastor, although saying, "You too" is often appropriate, but it could indicate some hysterical features to the person being seen. Another response by the person can be the introduction of something new with the opening phrase "by the way." This maneuver on the part of the person is not seen as an attempt to cling to the pastor or the session, but more an attempt to drop something that is "hot" and then run. Material introduced with "by the way" contains ambivalent elements which the person doesn't want to face yet, but which she or he wants the pastor to know about. Sometimes the person gives the material as a means of testing out the pastor's response. However important the material may seem to the pastor, he should note it and then raise it at a later interview, generally the next one. This kind of ambivalent material is important data. If the pastor delays the termination of the session in an attempt to deal with it, the person will not be inclined to test out other dangerous material in this way again.

Sometimes as a person goes out the door she or he will ask for an assurance in such a way: "Do you think you can help?" This can be handled somewhat like Sullivan (1954) did when he said something to the effect, "For gosh sakes, it's a tall order to give a definite yes or no." The question may also be approached by the pastor responding that he needs the other evaluation sessions before he can give any kind of intelligent response to that kind of question.

In pastoral therapy, once regular appointments have been made, the person may ask for an extra session as she or he goes out the door. This can be an indirect way of complaining about the ineffectiveness of the session that has just been held. It is best to deal with this request by the "next time" move. If the pastor senses that there is real urgency behind the request, she or he may suggest that the person phone the next day for an extra appointment if the person still feels the same way. The bind of the pastor is that if there is any delay in the ending of of the session this fact may be interpreted as signaling that the person is something special. Thus by saying, "Let's talk about it next time," the pastor avoids giving that message, but still puts herself or himself into the position of dealing with the request at the first possible moment in which time can be taken to explore the meaning of the request. Naturally, all of the person's behavior after the pastor has announced that time is up needs to be carefully noted and recorded in the write-up for supervision and for diagnostic purposes.

The final source of data on the person seeking help comes from the pastor's own feelings. In any write-up the pastor's feelings about the person need to be included. Known to contain the presenting transference, these data are valuable because the pastor, as an agent of pastoral care or as pastoral therapist, is not just a scientific observer. The pastor is what Harry Stack Sullivan calls a "participant observer." By participation it is meant that the pastor's feelings get involved if there is any real engagement with the person seeking help.

Countertranference as a source of data for the presenting transference presupposes that the pastor is in touch with her or his own feelings. Unfortunately, this is not always the case, especially where the pastor has obsessive-compulsive dynamics and these dynamics have been reinforced by a heavy dose of overintellectualized theology. To counteract this completely rational approach to theological education in seminaries, the clinical pastoral education (C.P.E.) movement has placed considerable emphasis on the feelings of the pastor doing pastoral care. Many a pastor now functioning in the parish can testify to the painful but worthwhile experience she or he had in a quarter of C.P.E. where the C.P.E. supervisor and/or peers in training confronted her or him until she or he started to recognize personal feelings in a pastoral care situation, such as a patient dying of cancer.

In stressing the value of countertransference feelings, there is always the danger that the pastor may be somewhat hysterical and have too many feelings herself or himself. Some of these feelings can get projected to the person seeking help and all kinds of distortions occur in the evaluation process. Again, while this is a danger, it is minimized through supervision and minimized when the pastor knows her or his own dynamics because of undergoing psychotherapy.

What the evaluation using the countertransference feelings depends on is the development of a reciprocity of feelings between the pastor and the person. Even in one session the person relates in such a way as to begin the development of some kind of symbiotic relationship most appropriate to the personality structure of herself or himself. The most well known of these symbiotic relationships is the dynamics related to hysteria. The female hysteric, for example, manages to sexualize the relationship so that the male pastor feels sexually aroused. This is not because the female hysteric is feeling sexual, but because of her anger, anxiety, or boredom. Nevertheless, sexual arousal is the male pastor's feeling which points to diagnosis of hysteria in the female seeking help.

Other examples of feelings that could point to a specific diagnosis follow.

Pastor's Feelings	Possible Diagnosis of the Person
Male pastor feels actually aroused by female person	Hysteria
Feeling used, manipulated	Sociopathic or narcissistic
Feeling guilty	Passive-dependent
Feeling annoyed, frustrated, and angry	Obsessive-compulsive or passive-aggressive
Feeling afraid	Schizophrenia, borderline syndrome or primary affective disorder
Feeling attacked or provoked	Paranoia

It perhaps needs to emphasized that these feelings are only pointers to the diagnosis indicated, although they are most valuable pointers. In general, the more experience the pastor has in using countertransference feelings, especially when they have been cross-checked by hundreds of hours of competent supervision, the more reliable they are. However, they also need to be checked against all of the other data being presented under the assumption held throughout this book that effective pastoral care and pastoral therapy depend more upon a sound, comprehensive methodology and painstaking observation in gathering of data, than on charismatic charm.

The pastor needs to write up the initial interview for his own private records or for supervision. In suggesting the format used in this book it is hoped that the pastor's write-up will help bring to light data that would otherwise be overlooked. The write-up where there is no supervision becomes a simple way for the pastor to keep a check on herself or himself. By stressing again the supervisory function of a write-up the reader is reminded that no one can learn effective pastoral care or pastoral therapy from a book, including this one. It has been the author's experience that the better the ability of the pastor to write-up, the better the pastoral care and/or pastoral therapy. Also, the more effective the pastoral care or pastoral therapy, the better the write-up. Thus in any training of pastors in effective pastoral care or therapy, it is hoped that a circular buildup or dialectic effect gets generated between write-up, supervision, and effective pastoral care and pastoral therapy.

Essentially, there are five types of writing with which a pastor serious about effective pastoral care and/or pastoral therapy ought to be familiar:

1. Initial interview
2. Verbatims
3. Process notes
4. Case conference summaries
5. Closing summaries

The difference between these various kinds of writing arise largely out of the nature and composition of the audience imagined and the use to which the materials will be put. Each of these distinctive types of writing is an attempt to objectify data that have come to the pastor subjectively. Each kind of writing is designed to reveal facts about persons, and in some cases, to interpret these facts. Each kind involves judgments as to what material to include and what to leave out.

In this chapter the first three types of writing will be discussed, leaving the other two for later chapters.

Initial Interview

The initial interview is written up in the style that has been systematically unfolding in chapters 1 and 2. Here, the parts will again be summarized.

1. Identifying Information
    Session No.
    Date
    Place
    Client—name, address, and phone number
    Pastor
2. Contact—how this was made
3. Description—age, marital status, height, weight, dress, facial features, gestures, voice, etc.
4. Initial behavior
5. Initial words
6. Presenting complaint or problem
7. Summary of the main points of the interview
8. Tentative contract for help
9. Termination material
10. Presenting countertransference—pastor's feelings
11. Tentative diagnosis—based on the presenting transference

This may seem a lot, but by using a structured outline like this a pastor can keep the initial interview write-up to approximately two pages of double-spaced typing.

Verbatims

Before the advent of video tapes and audio tapes, verbatims were an essential part of helping pastors become more proficient at doing pastoral care or pastoral therapy. As a form of writing, verbatims are on the decline, except in special parts of an interview. The special parts follow.

1. The first few words

2. The last words where these words occur after the statement by the pastor "our time's up now"
3. If a crisis occurs during the interview
4. Phrases that stand out in the memory

Regarding a possible overuse of verbatims in some pastoral care programs it would be well for the pastor to heed these words of Sullivan (1954):

"A verbatim record of an interview, until it has been heavily annotated is almost invariably remarkably misleading. I have had some recordings of interviews which I regarded as astonishingly good teaching material, but when I have sprung these on intelligent colleagues, I have often found them barking up trees that I haven't seen, if, indeed, such trees were ever there, and I can't realize that they weren't. In other words, the complete meaning of the conversation is not to be found in the verbatim verbal context of the communication, but is reflected in all sorts of subtle interplay."

Process Notes
There is a close similiarity between the initial interview and the process note. The intake interview is a special form of the process note. Theoretically, everything that is material for the intake interview is also material for the process note. In practice, however, it is only changes in description, behavior, the contract, and the diagnosis that need to be noted. The pastor should always try to get a verbatim of the first few words. Sometimes the last few words of the interview are also worth noting. The principal part of the process note consists of the main points presented in the session and the way the pastor handled this material, including the perception of any feelings involved of both the person and the pastor. Remember, this material is meant for the supervisor, is very subjective, and sometimes "personal." It is not intended for general reading and is often written in haste. Nevertheless, the process note, because it attempts to follow the order, or process, of the pastoral care or pastoral therapy, is the basic unit for the whole case.

An example of a complete initial process note follows.

Write-up No. 8

Identifying Information

    Session: No. 1

    Date: August 4, 1975

    Place: First Methodist Church, Evanston, Illinois

    Client: Mrs. Brown

          2689 Asbury Avenue

          Evanston, Illinois 60201

          Phone: 869-2511

    Pastor: John Doe

Contact: This initially was made by a third party, a fellow parishioner. Mrs. Brown then phoned for an appointment and said she was having "family difficulties."

Description: Mrs. Brown is a very attractive woman, 40 years of age, about 5'8" tall and weighing 160 lb. She wore a short, stylish green skirt, matching blouse and hose, and new looking shoes. Her carefully made up face was so tense it looked as if she were in physical pain. She seldom looked at the pastor directly. When she spoke her voice quivered with emotion and she repeatedly used the gesture of "fixing her hair."

Initial Behavior: Mrs. Brown sat on a hard chair near the door, but after a few moments moved to a comfortable couch, where she lit a cigarette and crossed her shapely legs.

Initial Words: "It was very kind of you to see me when I am not one of your parishioners."

Presenting Complaint or Problem: Her husband was spending more time with his parents than with her.

Main Summary of Material: Mrs. Brown indicated her husband slept at his parents' house about twice a week. She further said that they seldom had sex anymore, and when they did it was not very successful because her husband made it an act of duty more than anything else. They had been married seven years; he had been affectionate and attentive at first, but now she couldn't understand his behavior at all.

    When asked if she was angry at being neglected, she said no, that she was more puzzled than anything else. And when asked why her husband should prefer his parents to her and his three children, Mrs.

Brown said she didn't know, but did admit she felt jealous at times, and this would lead to some nagging behavior on her part. She claimed that the mother-in-law interfered too much in their family life. When asked to give an example, she stated that the mother-in-law was always baking special treats to entice her son back to her. Mrs. Brown said her children were always disobedient after they returned from a visit with "Grandma."

It was eventually pointed out to Mrs. Brown that this problem had been going on for a long time. When asked if there was anything that made the problem worse at this time which led her to seek help, she replied that for some reason she had reached the stage where she "just couldn't stand it any longer."

Contract: Mrs. Brown was asked what she was expecting by way of help. Without hesitation she said she hoped that the pastor would visit their house and talk to her husband about staying at his mother's place as much as he did. It was pointed out to her that his asking her husband to do this would probably have little affect except antagonize him and his family. He suggested she come back next week at the same time to explore the possibilities. When she agreed, he also suggested that she think about spending an extra session or two giving details on her background and this she readily agreed to do as well as take some tests.

Termination of Session: Just as Mrs. Brown reached the door she said, "By the way, my husband has been receiving calls from an unknown woman." This was handled by the pastor saying, "Let's discuss this next time."

Presenting Countertransference: "I felt mildly sexually aroused by her attractive looks and seductive behavior. I felt under pressure to help this "damsel in distress."

Tentative Diagnosis: Hysterical features seem prominent; paranoid and narcissistic possibilities need further exploration.

In writing up this case the pastor revealed his training. He followed an approach often used in clinical circles and recommended by Draperetal

---

*Pastor Doe had been supervised by a qualified therapist on several cases before. He decided to go ahead and evaluate and then get a consultation. Marriage or even family counseling, including in-laws, could be an option after this if it was deemed advisable.

(1965). He has monitored the material given by the person by looking for answers to these three questions.

1. Why does the person come?
2. Why does the person come now?
3. Why does the person come now to me?

Many pastors would be far more effective in their work if they used this format during the initial interview whether for pastoral care or pastoral therapy.

3 : Evaluation Process

The primary purpose of an evaluation is to devise a strategy for change. Evaluating is more than an initial task for the pastoral therapist; it is her or his continuing task throughout the therapy. To make the therapy more effective the pastoral therapist is always evaluating the material of sessions with a view to testing out and modifying the initial evaluation and hence is constantly open to changing the initial treatment strategy and the tactics (techniques) which evolve from that strategy.

Having given presenting transference considerable attention in chapters 1 and 2, the next step is to look at the matter of taking a history with a view to incorporating its data into a more complete evaluation. The procedure recommended here is generally to start the history at the beginning of the second session. However, the pastoral therapist should exercise considerable flexibility in deciding when to take a history. If the person has clearly presented herself or himself including her or his problem, before the end of the first session, the pastoral therapist may want to start taking the history during the first session. On the other hand, sometimes it may be necessary to delay taking a history for several sessions, because only after the person has talked herself or himself out, and gained some emotional relief and/or trust, will she or he be ready to answer questions related to a personal history. This could be because the person comes to the pastor for immediate relief and has to be helped to see that there may be underlying reasons why problems are arising. The suggestion to the person to have a history taken often serves the purpose of helping focus that person on the possibility of underlying dynamics behind the immediate psychic pain. On the other hand, many persons come to the pastor who conducts pastoral therapy with minor pastoral care problems which can be handled on a "one shot" basis, so that delaying the history taking until the second session enables pastoral care to continue without the interference of a more thorough evaluation approach.

The procedure advocated here is essentially a compromise between two positions. One, practiced in clinics, uses the initial session as an "intake" with a social worker generally taking a history. On the other hand, there is the opposite position that it is not necessary to take a history at all. The author evolved the position advocated in this book through his practice of pastoral therapy and pastoral care in a parish context, not in a pastoral counseling center. The procedure allowed him to contact many persons on an informal or one-session basis and, at the same time allowed the possibility eventually of obtaining a history and making a more thorough evaluation in order to deepen his pastoral care work or make more effective referrals. It also enabled him to be able to contract with some for pastoral therapy when this was appropriate.

Skill is required to take a personal history, or else this work can easily deteriorate from a meaningful, dynamic interaction into a dull, mechanical, question-and-answer session. *The pastor needs to resist any compulsive tendencies to take a thorough, in-depth history on a person at this time*. It is better to take what Harry Stack Sullivan refers to as a "reconnaissance" through all the essential facets of a person's life. In this way the history taking points to the trouble spots which will emerge during the course of the pastoral therapy and which can be explored in depth at a later session. The history also contains invaluable data from which to create a dynamic formulation.

The following are key areas to cover in taking a history are (Christensen 1952).

Family history	Medical history
Birth and early development	Social history
Educational history	Religious history
Sexual development	Mental Status
Habits and routines	Special questions
Occupational history	

It is not essential that these areas be followed in any strict or rigid pattern. Nor is it essential that all of one area be covered before another is explored. Many persons being interviewed will jump around frequently and the skillful pastoral therapist not only permits this, but fosters as much spontaneity in the history taking as possible, even if this means more than one session is needed for history-taking purposes. Generally some history material is mentioned in the initial session without being elicited. Skillful history takers are able to pick up on these points in the second and/or third session and use them naturally as a way of opening up further questions.

Sometimes a person will answer the immediate question with the material sought, but then launch into associations. Such associative material, while often not related directly to what the history taker wants to know, is extremely valuable and ought not be discouraged unless the process threatens to drag out the reconnaisance beyond three sessions. When history taking is undertaken in this manner, more than half of the material may be offered without direct questioning by the pastor, thus turning her or his role eventually into one of steering the person towards the untouched areas or gaps.

Family History
Opening up the subject of the person's family is generally not difficult. The pastor can generally say something like, "You were mentioning your mother (father) a few minutes ago (or last session). What is she (he) like?" If the response of the person is to talk about how well she or he gets along with each parent, the pastor can eventually ask for some factual details such as age, birth order, occupation, and education. If, however, the person gives factual data about parents, the pastor can ask about the personal relationship with each parent. In finding out how well the person does or does not "get along" with each parent, the pastor needs to ask for an example of some transaction of the person with each parent to illustrate what she or he means. These examples can be very revealing.

The actual data about a family can alert a pastor to many important matters that need to be explored at a later time. For example, in one situation where a 44-year-old person came for help from the pastor because of an anxiety attack, the astute pastor noted to himself that the man's father died of an accident at the age of 44, in front of the son's eyes. At a later session, the pastor was able to help this man explore his feelings of guilt at the prospect of surviving beyond the length of time his father lived.

Just asking for the age and the relationships of various family members will often uncover a great deal. Divorces, deaths, and birth order will sometimes point to a lot of family and personal pain. In fact, in having the person talk about her or his family, the pastor will find she or he is very quickly swamped with material. To keep a lot of this clear the pastor is advised to diagram the family during the session. In one useful system squares denote men and circles, women. A dotted circle or square indicates a death. A horizontal line between a couple indicates marriage, while a dotted horizontal line means a divorce. A vertical line represents sibling relationships. The present age of each person in the diagram is placed inside the circle or square. Where there has been a death, the year the person died and the age at the time of death is placed inside the circle or square. See Diagram 1 for a sample of this kind of family diagramming.

The person seeking help (indicated by the shaded square in the diagram) divorced the 42-year-old woman 10 years ago when their oldest son was 10 years old. This son is now married with a one-year-old son of his own. Eight years ago, when he was 37, the person married a 21-year-old woman and they now have three children. The birth order indicates that the person, as an oldest child, first married another eldest child. (One would anticipate dominance conflicts (Toman 1961). Then in his second marriage he married a youngest child.

The diagram also shows that the person's father died at the age of 45, when the person was 10 years of age. His present wife's grandmother is still living at age 88. His wife's brother is divorced and her sister is single. Thus, it can be seen how much valuable information can be contained in such a diagram, and that the more complex the family and extended relationships, the more necessary it becomes to have something like this to clarify matters. Names, educational background, and occupations would add much more.

When the presenting problem has to do with the person's mood, particularly depression, the family section of the history taking becomes crucial to the diagnosis. In the last decade considerable progress has been made in discovering biochemical components to unipolar (Winokur 1969) and bipolar primary affective disorders (PAD). Suicidal thoughts or attempts, and previous hospitalization for depression with or without electro convulsive therapy (ECT) are pointers to the possibility of this syndrome (Greene 1976). Another way the syndrome can be uncovered is through tracing the incidence of the disease across generations (Fieve et al 1975). Sometimes the depression is masked in some way, particularly in the form of alcoholism.

The following is an example of how a pastor handled a case involving depression. A 43-year-old teacher presented himself as having a marital problem. He was having affairs, was not comfortable with his behavior, yet he did not want to stop. Furthermore, he felt he couldn't leave his

Date Taken: *June 1976*

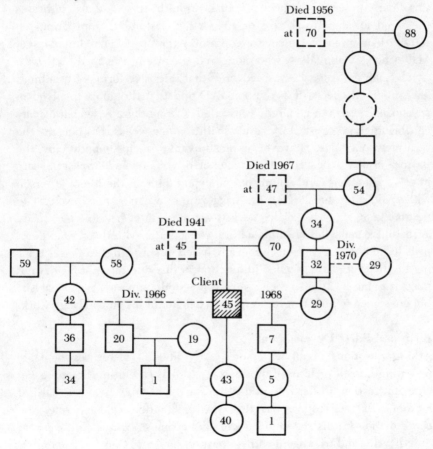

Diagram 1. *A Family History Diagram*

wife despite periods of intense depression. Through the history the pastor discovered that the man's father had been hospitalized for depression, sometimes for weeks. The teacher's brother also had periods of severe depression. In discussing this matter with the person's wife, she related to the pastor without knowing what he was seeking, that their teenage daughter also had some depressive episodes. While the pastor did not attempt to make a diagnosis of a PAD, he felt there was enough evidence to warrant a psychiatric referral, through which his diagnosis was confirmed.

The person with a PAD syndrome is deliberately mentioned because this clearly indicates the necessity of a careful history, and also indicates the need for a pastoral care or supportive pastoral therapy approach rather than intensive uncovering pastoral therapy. Since the days of Mabel Blake Cohn (1954) who pioneered the attempt to treat PAD with psychoanalysis, it has been discovered that intensive forms of treatment have minimal effects, if any, upon PAD and that the effort involved in psychoanalysis is not generally warranted. Chemotherapy, which usually can bring about satisfactory results within a few weeks, has become the treatment of choice. However, as an adjuvant to such chemotherapy, the pastor's ability to be available to such persons on demand for pastoral care in crisis situations can be a major stabilizing force in the life of a person with PAD, often heading off the triggering of a major mood cycle. The pastor's knowing of her or his flock, trust built up over years, and ready availability, make her or him a natural collaborator with the chemotherapists in helping prevent biochemically based mood swings from devastating the lives of many people. To function in this role the pastor does not need training in intensive uncovering psychotherapy or psychoanalysis, but does need to be caring and supportive in her or his pastoral care work.

Birth and Early Development
Asking questions about a person's early life can foster resistance to revealing herself or himself unless the pastor is careful in the approach. One suggestion is for the pastor to start with the person's earliest memory. If the response is that she or he doesn't have one, the contradiction in this statement generally becomes obvious. If the pastor quietly waits and tries again with a question such as, "Can you remember anything when you were about 10?" and the person responds in the affirmative (usually the case), the pastor can start working backwards asking

for a description of an earlier memory until reaching the earliest one the person can recall. Whether the memory is virtually true or a projected event (screen memory), the earliest memory is often an important window into the unconscious mind of the person.

In a similar fashion the family lore surrounding the person's birth can be important data. Did the mother suffer a deep postpartum depression beyond the "three days blues"? Was the birth cesarean or the labor difficult in any way? Was the person bottle or breast fed? Did any traumatic events occur to the family involving major changes soon after the person's birth? In general, what the pastor looks for is evidence concerning the person's upbringing in a stable, consistant "good-enough" mothering environment (Winnicott 1966).

In taking a history the pastor is advised to know something about the early stages of development, especially as interpreted by thinkers such as Harry Stack Sullivan, Erik Erikson (1950), Donald Winnicott, or Margaret Mahler et al (1975). In the oral-trust stage, the death or absence of the mother can have a traumatic impact on the infant. In the anal-autonomy stage, the pastor is interested in how the person experienced the attempt of the mother world to modify her or his wishes and foster feelings that she or he is a special person. Feeding, walking, toilet training, and language formation are examples of important areas to look at for clues about a person's earlier experiences and response to them. Difficulties in toilet training and late talking point to the possible expression of anger over the way the person was treated as an infant. There are, of course, many things that could be helpful to know about, but feeding, toilet training, walking, and talking tend to be areas of socialization a person is most likely to remember or know something about.

Educational History
By education it is meant that everything from grade school to graduate school is covered in a swift reconnaissance. In grade school the question about liking it seems to best get at the material in the preadolescent period. It is also worth asking if the person remembers her or his first day at school and then to describe it. Questions about grades and the subjects in which the person did well or poorly while in high school or university also can be very productive. How involved in extracurricular activities and how well liked the person was by peers helps broaden the scholastic picture. Being detained an extra year in a class, being expelled from

school, and shifting college frequently are examples of behavior that suggest a person struggling to cope with the academic system.

Sexual Development

Pastors often find taking a sexual history difficult at first, either because they have not come to terms with their own sexuality or because the parishioner sees the pastor in an unexpected role. While the area may be a sensitive one for either or both pastor and person, it is full of rich data and can often be a window into important intrapsychic conflicts. Asking questions about sexual development should not occur too early in the history-taking process. Nor should they be continued if the person becomes too upset (Chessick 1974); the reason for being upset can be explored at a later session. Nevertheless, the pastor will gain considerable insight into a woman's relationship with her mother, for example, by asking about how she, the person, found out about menstruation and what were the attitudes of the household towards this subject. Questions about dating are also useful to ascertain the breadth of experience during adolescense and young adulthood, and they offer a way of preparing the person for more explicit sexual questions such as the frequency of intercourse and the person's capacity to have orgasm. Naturally, the pastor needs to be calm and quietly detached as these questions are asked so as not to give the person any impression of "voyeurism." Information about premarital and extramarital sex is particularly useful for detecting the hypomanic behavior of a person with PAD. Again, while sexual behaviors can act as a pointer toward self-destructive, acting-out behavior, they may be difficult to obtain and should not be aggressively sought if the pastor's denomination is disapproving of this behavior. Masturbation fantasies can point to important unconscious processes in the mind, so can be worth the asking. Also, based on the experiences of Bernard Greene (1970), the pastor would find it well worth his while to ask about the courting and honeymoon experiences of the person if she or he is married. The question of any possible homosexual experiences also needs to be raised.

Habits and Routines

This section of exploration appears to be innocent enough and is often welcome by the person being treated as a relief from the anxiety of questioning about sex. The person is simply asked to describe a typical day in her or his life. It may surprise the pastor how quickly this question tends to uncover the richness or poverty of the person's life. A question like this, for example, is intended to unearth the rituals of the compulsive person and the excessive drinking behavior of the alcoholic. Smoking, eating, and drug habits should be explored as well.

Occupational History

The value of a work record is generally obvious. A person with 18 jobs over a 10-year-span, as happened in one case, obviously raises a question of why. Sometimes the person is able to be honest, but even where this is not so, the pastor can gain insight into the person's capacity to rationalize through questioning frequent job changes. Through a question like, "How did you get along with your bosses?" the pastor can pinpoint authority conflict. Another thing to evaluate is whether the job matches the person's education and experience, because a job well below the person's capacity begs for an explanation later on.

Medical History

It has been the experience of the author that many pastors are reluctant to ask for a medical history. As long as the pastor does not try to do a medical diagnosis herself or himself, thereby taking on a medical role, there are many good reasons why the pastor should note any illnesses that a medical practioner has already diagnosed. Asthma, diabetes, peptic ulcers, migraine, ulcerative colitis, and other diseases are all pointers to personality characteristics. If the pastor is not familiar with the psychological components to these and other illnesses he ought to consult the classic book *Psychosomatic Medicine* by Franz Alexander (1950) and one written specifically for the pastor (Young and Meiburg 1960). While the pastor is taking the medical history of the person seeking help, it can also be advantageous to ask about the medical history of her or his parents and other significant persons in the family.

Social History

A social history not only covers all the organizations to which the person belongs, including political ones, but moves into recreational activities and hobbies. The healthy person has a capacity to play and make sure that there is time for it. This is important for the pastor to keep in mind because so many "good" church people are "workaholics" and this portion of the material points clearly to a need in the person's life.

Religious History

In many history-taking procedures a religious history is subsumed under social history. But the pastor, because of his background, training, and sensitivity to religious issues, needs to make this a separate section. Following the work of Draper, et al (1965) pastors can find it revealing to ask questions like the following:

1. What is your favorite Bible story?
2. What is your favorite Bible verse?
3. What is your favorite Bible character?
4. If God were to grant you any three wishes, what would they be?
5. What is God like as you experience him?
6. What was your earliest religious experience?

These questions use the rich imagery of the Bible to penetrate into the fantasy side of the person's personality. Other data, such as the frequent shifting of the person's church membership, religious behavior of parents as compared with the person, regularity of attendance at worship, avoidance of the sacrament of the Lord's Supper (Mass, Eucharist) and many other matters can help flesh out the picture of the person the pastor is dealing with.

Mental Status

Without being too technical, it is invaluable for the pastor to make some judgments about the person as she or he functions in four areas (the questions included in the areas discussed are not asked of the person in therapy).

1. Intelligence: Is it high, average, or low? The pastor can gain an impression about the person's intelligence from the vocabulary used, the grasp of the questions, and the versatility of thought and knowledge.
2. Sensorium: This is a judgment the pastor can make as to the person's ability to know her or his own name, where she or he is, and what time it

is. The traditional way of talking about this is in terms of whether the person is "oriented to time, place, and person."

3. Memory: Does the person's memory appear to be defective in any way?

4. Affect: Was the affect during the history taking appropriate? Is the person "high" or depressed? Are there suicidal thoughts? What way does the person seem to express affection and anger?

Special Questions

Under this heading the pastor can ask questions such as whether the person being treated has any repetitive dreams. It sometimes pays the pastor to ask if there has been any question that the person has been expecting the pastor to ask and she or he hasn't done so yet. This will often unearth some unexpected but valuable information. This is also the time when the pastor may ask whether the person has been to see other professionals at any time to seek help and to discuss with the person what she or he expects from a helping relationship.

Like any good reconnaissance this outline of history taking covers a lot of ground fast. All sections or questions will not be of equal importance for all persons, so the history will be brief in some sections and fuller in others. For example, a housewife who is a faithful church attender did not have an occupational history worth mentioning, didn't drink or smoke, had a dull daily routine, and never involved herself in any outside social or recreational activities except church. It was the sexual history and the religious history which had the best material. Another person, on the other hand, can spend a great deal of time talking about sexual activities and drinking capers but say little in the religious section. All of this indicates the life-style of the person presenting herself or himself through the history.

The evaluation process is illustrated in the following write-up of a selected case. To be more thorough, the initial interview has been included before giving the history, but the headings have been discarded since the structure is clear from preceding chapters.

Write-up No. 9

Initial Session, Oct 21, 1977

First Methodist Church, Irving, Michigan

Client: Ms. Doe
      12 Broadway Avenue
      Irving, Michigan
      Phone: DA 6-6336
Pastor: Joe Smith

Ms. Doe, a member of the pastor's church, phoned for an appointment. She was having problems "accepting herself," she said.

Ms. Doe is a 5'3"-tall woman 26 years of age with rust colored hair but a body about 50 lb overweight. Her expensive looking, freshly pressed suit matched her hair which was neatly in place because she had just come from her hairdresser. Her voice was pitched high as she spoke. She smoked frequently during the session.

On entering the office Ms. Doe moved to the offered chair and quickly crossed her legs after sitting down. She said, "Is it alright if I light a cigarette?" She indicated she was becoming increasingly concerned about her low self-image.

She said that she was sensitive about her weight and had been having some conflict with her boy friend. She felt that some of her problems arose because she tried to control everything. She said that she had difficulty expressing her feelings and when she liked someone she couldn't say so. Instead, she became sarcastic and the person she liked then ended up not liking her.

The pastor contracted for two or three more sessions to evaluate the situation further. In going out the door Ms. Doe warned the pastor that she would be difficult to work with because of her intellectual defenses.

During the session the pastor felt some pressure to aid a "helpless maiden."

His initial tentative diagnosis was depressive neurosis in a hysterical personality.

Session: No. 2
Date: October 28, 1977

Ms. Doe smiled and confidently sat in the chair. She indicated she felt better after last week's session. She again reiterated that her relationship with her boy friend had reached a plateau and she feared she dominated him.

Family History: As Ms. Doe did not have anything urgent to relate in this session the pastor asked questions about her history. He diagrammed a good deal of information as shown in Diagram 2.

Date Taken: *June 1976*

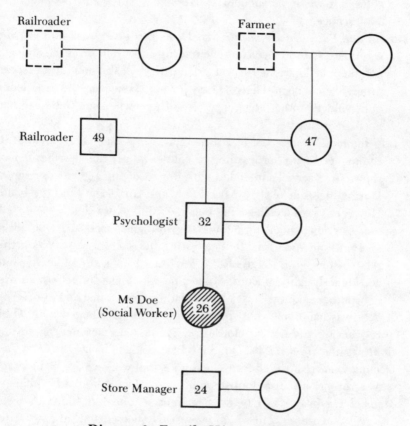

Diagram 2. *Family History of Ms Doe*

Ms. Doe was the middle of three children, with a 32-year-old married brother who was a psychologist and a 24-year-old married brother who was a store manager. Her 49-year-old father, a railroader and a son of a railroader, and her 47-year-old mother, daughter of a farmer, grew up together in the same rural town where they now live. The maternal and paternal grandparents who had resided in the same town, were now deceased.

Ms. Doe said she still visited her parents during vacations and also spent time staying in the homes of her brothers. She said she was closer to her mother than her father with whom she had not been able to have a meaningful conversation since the beginning of adolescence.

Birth and Early Development: Ms. Doe's birth had been normal. She was breast fed and given lots of cuddling and attention as the only girl grandchild. Learning to eat, defecate, speak, and other social processes had been relatively easy for her. However, the experience of her elder brother going into convulsions when she was small had been traumatic.

Educational History: Ms. Doe's academic career had been excellent. It commenced with her learning to count and say the alphabet before she went to school and ended with her receiving a graduate degree. During high school she was active in the Girl Scouts and the band. However, during college she became 70 lb overweight.

Sexual Development: After a few dates in high school, Ms. Doe fell in love with an American Indian during her college stay. When this relationship fell through after a few months she threw herself into getting a straight A record. Sometime after this she met a man who her mother said was "just like her father when I married him." This date was handsome, but so passive that she dominated him. Their relationship did not develop into a "physical experience."

Routines and Habits: Ms. Doe loved to cook and eat.

Occupational History: Besides being a social worker, she had worked as a receptionist at a dentist's office and as an aide in a hospital.

Medical History: Ms. Doe was so muscle tense at times that she developed a back pain which eventually necessitated surgery. Later she had another operation. She also continued to have a weight problem.

Social History: While Ms. Doe did not involve herself in many social activities, she always had several close girl friends.

Religious History: Ms. Doe's parents were members of the Christian Church, but she joined the Methodist Church as a teenager through the influence of her girl friend and a church youth group.

Mental Status: Ms. Doe used the language of a well-educated and intelligent person. She was oriented to time, place, and person. She responded to questions with appropriate affect.

Having this material available raised the question of how the presenting and history material could be integrated into a meaningful summary. The person being evaluated also had taken the Wechsler Adult Intelligence Scale (WAIS) and the Minnesota Multiphasic Personality Inventory (MMPI) tests, so more data was added to the summary. It needs, perhaps, to be said again that pastors are generally not trained to give such personality tests, nor are these tests necessary for an evaluation. However, where data from them are available, it is desirable to include them in the final evaluation summary, referred to as the dynamic formulation.

WAIS (Wechsler Adult Intelligence Scale): Ms. Doe scored in the very superior range of intelligence (I.Q. 137) with no significant difference between the verbal and performance subscales.

MMPI (Minnesota Multiphasic Personality Inventory): Ms. Doe presents as a person with a depressive neurosis in a hysterical personality, but this classic picture is modified in several ways. There is no significant overt depression; rather the depression comes out in the masked forms of mild acting-out and somatization. The acting-out is subtle and only takes place when she does not need the approval of others, or it takes place vicariously by identification with those who are willing to rebel against social norms and customs. Sometimes, when frustrated, she is prone to make hasty decisions, often without follow-through. The hysterical personality structure, while evident, is a mild form without an open and flagrant need for attention. This is partly because she has gained recognition and satisfaction through academic achievement. It is also because it became channeled into leadership roles. Ms. Doe is an ambitious, resourceful, and adaptable person, with good ego strength and well able to bounce back from adversity. This modifies to some extent the picture of sexual conflict and basic distrust of men.

The psychodynamic summary of a case generally includes some of the following elements.

Main conflicts
Primary source of anxiety

Chief defenses

Ego strength estimation

Prognosis

Disposition (This includes the action recommended, such as referral or therapy. If it is therapy, the type of therapy and goals of treatment need to be mentioned.)

In write-up no. 9 the dynamic formulation would look something like the following.

Main Conflicts
1. Her fear of intimacy seen in her relationship with her boy friend and her overweight, *versus* her fear of isolation seen in her need for medical attention
2. Her need for independence seen in her academic achievements and her strong career ambitions, *versus* her need for dependence as seen in her "oral" hunger
3. Her need to express anger seen in her identification with those rebelling against social law, *versus* her need for approval from parental surrogates seen in the academic mentors

Primary Sources of Anxiety: A growing sense of anger as the family dynamics are repeated in her work situation

Chief Defenses
1. Denial
2. Somatization
3. Acting-out
4. Reaction formation
5. Intellectualization

Ego Strength: Excellent (intelligence high, ego strength scales on the MMPI high)

Prognosis: Good

Disposition: Refer to a therapist for intensive, uncovering individual psychotherapy.

In this case the pastor was not trained to do such psychotherapy so the question of whether he could work with such a person and what the treatment strategy would be, was avoided. However, if the pastor had been trained as a pastoral therapist specialist, and was contemplating working with this person she or he would need to assess her or his capacity to establish a working alliance. A useful way of doing this is to ask three questions raised by Carl Rogers.

1. Is she or he able to offer congruency in the relationship whereby her or his nonverbal and verbal communication give a consistant communication?
2. Could she or he give this person unconditional positive regard?
3. Could she or he listen to this person, gain understanding, and then communicate the understanding back?

If the answer to any of these questions is no or maybe, it could be a contraindication for working with her. One reason for this stress on the pastoral therapist assessing whether she or he can work with a person is the knowledge that some cases get worse and not better under individual psychotherapy (Bergin 1970, Braucht 1970). If there are risks in psychotherapy, every effort needs to be made to reduce them to a minimum.

If the pastoral therapist, after evaluating the person and assessing her or his feeling of comfort about the idea of working with the person, decides to undertake therapy, she or he needs to go ahead and outline the treatment plan. As Carl Christensen (1952) indicates, a treatment plan is, in reality, little more than "working out a way of relating so you don't reinforce the patient's neurosis." The way the author likes to actually achieve this is by sitting down and thinking up ways that would make the person more dysfunctional or at least insure that she or he never changes. This helps sharpen the key problems and then enables the author to go about trying to do the very opposite to what would make the person sicker. For example, in the last write-up, one of the ways to insure that there would be no change would be to allow a great deal of intellectualization and acting-out to occur. Therefore, to effect change it would be important to watch for and interpret acting-out so that feelings are not drained off and become unavailable to the therapeutic sessions.

In chapter 2 it was stated that there were five types of clinical writing, but only three were enumerated then. What goes into an evaluation process has been sufficiently covered at this point to discuss the fourth of these writings, the case conference summary. Actually, write-up no. 9 is the summary of material that would be presented at a special kind of case conference called "staffing," which generally occurs in a pastoral counseling center, although it could also occur at a church.

The usual case conference summary contains material from more than two sessions and is generally presented because it raised issues, illuminates some aspect of theory, or is very instructive to other therapists. Hence, unlike other writings (verbatims, process notes, and intakes) that are for private use, the case conference summary is done with a projected audience in mind and has a potential audience in other places or in later years. This means the writer must take pains to engage in a variety of devices which could be summed up by the word "disguise." Disguise has been used in this book for all of the clinical writings, but would normally only be used for case conference summaries. It must be done with such skill that it does not distort the essential facts or interfere with clinical assessment.

The normal length of time for a case conference is from an hour to and hour and a half. The resistance to a case conference being longer can be understood, not only from the point of view that most professionals are busy people, but also from the fact that anywhere from six to 20 professionals in a conference means that a lot of time and money is involved. Therefore, the essential task of a case presentation is to distill into one paper all of the essential information, and present this information in such a way that most of the case conference time can be used in discussing dynamics, interpretations, strategy, and theoretical implications of the case. For practical reasons then, a case needs to be presented in six or seven pages. There is no infallible rule on this, but the longer the case material becomes, the more one risks giving the participants of the conference intellectual indigestion. Of course, if the case is particularly rich in material, sometimes extra length is appropriate.

Another factor influencing the length of the case will be the number of therapy sessions to be summarized. Usually, it takes at least two sessions before there is enough material for a case conference, and it could be possible for these sessions to be presented in about three pages. On the other hand, therapy may have gone for 30 or more sessions, and this fact may push the number of pages up to eight or nine. As a rough guide for a 20-session case, about half of the space would be spent on the first three or four sessions, and the other half of the case conference summary space would cover the remaining sessions.

Staffing is an important part of the evaluation process because it gives a chance for the pastoral therapist to have her or his evaluation tested out with other therapists as a further attempt to bring as much experience to bear on the treatment strategy as possible. Staffing also gives the pastoral therapist a chance to test out possible countertransference feelings.

After staffing, where the pastoral therapist has firmed her or his evaluation of the person in therapy, the person needs to be informed of as much of this evaluation as possible, particularly aspects that would be of immediate use. This is done in an interpretative session. Generally, the person comes with heightened anxiety to such a session because of hurting in some way. Also, she or he often irrationally hopes that in some magical way something will be said that will immediately change her or him. Therefore, a discourse in theory or use of technical terms is undesirable.

Pastors learning to give interpretations generally find the task extremely difficult and often report feeling as if they were judging the person. Sometimes they are so anxious about the role that they "dump" all the material in on long discourse on the person seeking help. Then, the more uncomfortable the person becomes the more the neophyte pastoral therapist resorts to technical language to reinforce her or his threatened authority. Under these circumstances the person experiences the interpretive session as a judgment where she or he is being "put down." Understandably, this process builds up immediate resistance in the person and undermines any potential good that might have come from the session or even later sessions.

Because of the abortive possibilities just mentioned, it is seriously suggested that the therapist focus on one major idea for a start and interpret this idea using ordinary language or, if possible, employing the very phrases used by the person herself or himself. By then waiting for a response it is possible to cue the person into understanding that this is going to be an interacting process rather than the final authoritative word delivered from "on high." Once the person responds, it is possible to give other pieces of the picture, each time allowing the person to respond and indicate how she or he feels about it. It is not unusual for the person to get so involved that she or he starts illustrating and reinforcing the interpretations. When this happens the interpretative sessions can be extremely effective in helping the person.

Naturally, everything given in the interpretative session will not bring forth agreement. In fact, it is considered excellent if the person seems to have understood about 80% of what has been said. In most cases, however, it is hoped that enough has been said and accepted to enable the person to start working on her or his hurts with some therapist, if not with the person giving the interpretation.

Sometimes the interpretative session also includes, for the pastor, the task of making a referral to another therapist. When this is so, the pastoral therapist needs to spend time in dealing with the feelings of the person about a referral and may necessitate setting up several further sessions to work on any resistances to the referral. Referral is discussed at some length in chapter 8.) Thus, the interpretative session becomes another potential referral point in the helping process, in addition to the other optimum referral points already mentioned in previous chapters, namely 1) during the contact and 2) at the end of the first session.

In some instances, despite considerable skill on the part of the pastor during the interpretative session, the person will get angry and defensive about what she or he has heard. When this occurs, the worst thing the pastor can do is to get into an angry and defensive argument whereby the pastor tries to justify her or his conclusions. Rather, it is better to say something like the following.

> "No human can be right 100% of the time, so I, Mrs. Cahan, may not be accurate in the case of your evaluation, but I have given this my best professional judgment and I am prepared to stand behind it."

Then the pastor should let the matter lie and allow the interpretation to continue the fermentation it has obviously produced. It also needs to be remembered that many practicing therapists have as high as a 60% attrition rate at the interpretation point in the helping process. The person may hurt and may think that she or he wants help, but if the person is not ready to deal with these hurts through significant change, it is better for her or him to be weeded out at this stage before she or he misspends much time, energy, and money.

If, on the other hand, a person accepts most of the interpretative material and seems ready to work on her or his problems, the next step is to establish a working contract. Such a working contract is psychological rather than legal in nature. As Harry Levinson (1962) explains it, "the psychological contract is a series of mutual expectations of which the parties to the relationship may not themselves be even dimly aware, but which nonetheless govern their relationship to each other." In setting up a working contract the pastoral therapist will need to make as clear as possible what she or he expects from the relationship, such as fees and time, length, and regularity of sessions, as well as missed sessions, vacations and other matters that define the structure of the relationship. Some pastoral therapists give an approximate idea of how long the therapy may take if the client works at it.

Care must be taken in discussing the nature of the working contract with a person that the pastor does not promise or imply any ability to cure. There is no such thing as perfect cure anymore than perfect justice or a perfect world. As Dr. Fried says to Deborah in *I never Promised You a Rose Garden* (Green 1964):

> "I never promised you a rose garden, I never promised you perfect justice."

> "And I never promised you peace or happiness. My help is so that you can be free to fight for all of these things. The only reality I offer is challenge, and being well is being free to accept it or not at whatever level you are capable. I never promised lies, and the rose garden world of perfection is a lie . . . and a bore, too!"

In undertaking pastoral therapy, then, the pastor has the task of not only clearly indicating what she or he expects by way of arrangements, but also of exploring with the person the expectations that the person brings to the therapy, with a view to modifying those that are unrealistic or impossible to fulfill. Clarifying the contract in the interpretative session and at any stage in the process of therapy where it seems necessary, will do much to foster a successful therapeutic outcome. On the other hand, many of the messes seen by supervisors have occurred because of fuzzy and unresolved contracting problems by the pastor.

One of the reasons why pastors get into contracting problems with people who are seeking help is because contracting takes place at various levels. As Kenneth Mitchell (1972) indicates, there are at least three levels of contracting: formal, informal, and tacit. Mitchell developed these ideas when thinking about the marital contract, but they can apply as well to other forms of psychological contracting, including individual pastoral psychotherapy. The formal contract is where the therapist indicates she or he would be willing to work with the person and the person indicates a desire to work with the therapist. This formal agreement generally takes place during the interpretative session.

The content of that agreement is really what Michell would call the informal contract which is open for negotiation and change during the course of the therapy without necessarily altering the formal agreement, that is, to the therapy itself. Components of the informal agreements are, as had been stated earlier, such matters as fees, the time of the meeting, and the length and number of sessions, all of which will be discussed in detail in the next chapter as structure. The tacit, or "secret", contract consists of the unconscious expectations of the client towards the therapist, and the therapist's unconscious expectations of the person to fulfill some of her or his personal needs. In the course of successful pastoral therapy these expectations get uncovered and dealt with. In cases where they remain unexamined misalliances (Lange 1976) develop and the therapeutic work is limited, if not aborted. Hence, while contracting takes place in the interpretative session, the contracting process and the examination of the contract is never complete until the case is terminated.

While the notion of contracting is being presented in the context of intensive, uncovering pastoral therapy, it is also of great importance for the pastor in her or his general ministry and pastoral care work. As Mitchell indicates, much of the pastor's work can be to help couples in premarriage counseling clarify the informal contracts. Also, a valuable approach to marriage counseling itself consists of helping to surface and identify unconscious contracts that are leading to marital conflicts.

In addition to its use in marriage counseling, the notion of contracting is important when a pastor is exploring a "call" to a church or is appointed to one by a bishop as is the case in the Methodist Church. In the United Church of Christ, Presbyterian, and Baptist denominations, for example, the need for a negotiating, contracting process is obvious, but it is contended here that in the Episcopal or appointive system there is still a lot more tacit contracting than is generally realized, and that the extent to which it is taking place is better surfaced and made a part of the informal contract than kept a part of the tacit, or unconscious contract. For example, in the hiring of a minister for a multiple-staff situation, some attempts at contracting occur when the search committee commences with a job description, or when the minister being appointed asks for one from the pastoral relations committee. The reason most often given for the procedure is the clarification of the roles of the various staff ministers. After working hard at formulating a clear and satisfactory job description, the matter is closed, generally with the pastor agreeing to come to the church or being appointed to it by the bishop. What has not been realized is that the job description is little more than a formal contract. The fact that the informal and tacit aspects of the contract are generally ignored helps explain why so many assistant or associate pastor positions with nice formal descriptions turn out to be a living hell!

Even if a committee appears to have an adequate job description there is generally a lot more to be done. The process is not adequately complete until both parties in a negotiating process are able to find out through informal discussions what it is exactly that the pastor really wants to do and what it is the church would really like to see accomplished. For these things to emerge it takes time and the building up of a great deal of trust which generally does not take place in an hour or two with one formal meeting of a search committee. By trying to get at wishes and wants, some of the unconscious fantasy life is tapped and the tacit contract will commence to emerge. In other words, knowledge of the three levels of contracting leads one beyond the traditional job description an assessment of the dynamic elements involved.

However, it is contended here that even if all of the hidden hopes and fears are surfaced from both sides of the negotiation, and the expectations are exceedingly clear and understood, contracting has still not gone far enough. Additionally, contracting involves an assessment of the other party's ability to meet the expectations involved. For example, a pastor may make it very clear in contracting to a church that she or he wants half a day a week off for her or his own continuing education purposes, and the church committee may understand this and agree. Yet the pastor could still eventually find herself or himself in trouble with the pastoral relations committee six months later, because with all of the other work expectations the committee had, there was no realistic way she or he could possibly ever get the half a day a week for continuing education purposes. In other words, the committee was not in a position to agree to the request because of the already unrealistic work-load expectations, and because they were not prepared to shift priorities. The pastor should not only have made the request for continuing education clear, but should have assessed the general workload to see whether the promise given was realistic or not. Contracting then, involves assessment of the capacity of both parties to meet the contract as well as clarifying the exact nature of that contract.

4 : Therapeutic Setting

A major responsibility of the pastoral therapist in working with a person is to provide an adequate therapeutic setting, often called a structure or frame. (Langs 1976.) By structure it is meant that a pastoral therapist sets up the ground rules of the relationship which involve such things as length, number and place of sessions, matter of fees, physical arrangements of the office, and behavior that can't be tolerated by the therapist. In saying that the major responsibility for structure rests with the pastoral therapist, it is meant that the therapist should make the final decision about these matters and hence is free to initiate a discussion of structural matters at any stage of the relationship when she or he feels the problems of the working alliance call for it. However, once the therapy is underway the person generally raises structural questions through behavior which tests the limits. Structural mattters are generally discussed first after the person has agreed to work with the pastor.

A pastor learning to be a therapist often has difficulty establishing the firm structure necessary for a working relationship. She or he fears that making structural decisions without consulting the client will cause her or him to seem too authoritarian. This fear, however, points to an unresolved autonomy issue in the pastor more than anything else. For most persons seeking help raise no issue about the pastoral therapist setting the structure, in fact, they generally welcome it as a "given."

There is a basic confusion in seeing the setting of structure as being authoritarian. To be authoritarian means to completely control a relationship, whereas the pastoral therapist taking responsibility for structure is really only making decisions for one element of the relationship, albeit, and important one. Furthermore, in the pastoral therapist's role of assuming responsibility for structural issues, there is the implicit message that absolute freedom doesn't exist. Hence, through the way the pastoral therapist handles the structural elements of a working relationship with the person seeking help, she or he is able to present a reality with which the person must deal in life itself. Rather than restrict freedom, the structural matters of therapy can be so handled that they maximize the freedom of the person seeking help.

A pastor who cannot be firm in setting up the structure of a helping relationship, for whatever reason, should not involve herself or himself in doing intensive pastoral therapy or should only do so after she or he has been through intensive, uncovering psychotherapy to resolve this need. Persons seeking help need structure, in a varying degree to be sure, but the need is great enough in most cases for Eric Berne (1969) to talk about "structure hunger." The need for structure is so basic, in fact, that if it is neglected, effective intensive, uncovering pastoral therapy cannot take place.

One of the functions of structure is to "bind anxiety." This binding effect is often seen at the time of contact where a person thinks she or he must see the pastor immediately, but where the pastor enforces some delay by setting up a later appointment. Often the very fact the person has an appointment is enough to start lowering anxiety and help her or him experience immediate relief. Another example of the binding effect of structure on anxiety is when a crisis occurs in the therapy and the person becomes more anxious. This can sometimes be successfully handled by having an extra session or two during the crisis, thus enabling the therapist to explore with the person the underlying dynamics behind the crises as well as help shore up the defenses temporarily.

Structural matters can be listed in many ways. Certainly, it is important for the therapist to discuss with the person the nature of the therapeutic sessions such as their length. The traditional length is 50 minutes, as is reflected in Lindner's fascinating book, *The Fifty Minute Hour* (1955). However, it should be noted that many therapists have reduced the "hour" to 45 minutes and others have experimented with more and less time for a session. For example, some marriage therapists find that conjoint sessions are better if they are one and a half hours. On the other hand, one study found that it was difficult to maintain the client-therapist relationship when the person was seen for only half an hour every two weeks. It seems, then, reasonable to assume that there are parameters to the length of sessions with the "law of diminishing returns" operating the longer a session, and a difficulty in maintaining the relationship operating the shorter or less frequently a session is held. Thus, the spacing of sessions can be a way to facilitate the weakening of the relationship when termination is the goal.

Sometimes a person may request two sessions a week when first seeking therapeutic help. The meaning behind this request needs to be explored carefully with the person. Often it means that she or he is expecting quick results or really doesn't want to be in therapy and wants to complete it as quickly as possible. It is important, in such a situation, to resist two sessions a week on the ground that it will generally not speed therapy, and at the same time explore carefully with the person the reason for the request. If anything, two sessions tend to prolong the therapy because the extra session fosters more regression. Yet, in attempting core characterological change, two sessions and the resulting regression are necessary if the defensive armor is to be penetrated. And, if a crisis occurs during brief therapy on a once-a-week basis, it may be necessary to temporarily increase the number of sessions to help bind the anxiety involved. In such a crisis it can be argued that the crisis has already fostered regression, and the extra weekly sessions are needed to support the person's defenses during this regressive period.

There is not a great deal known about the effects of the broader setting of the place of therapy, that is, outside of the office itself. However, of interest to pastors is the study done by Seward Hiltner and Lowell Colston (1961) where church persons seeking counseling were randomly assigned to be seen by pastors in both a clinic and church setting. While this was not a tightly controlled experiment, the conclusion was that the results of therapy were better in the church. It was assumed that the context of therapy had an effect on the interaction. Although this conclusion could possibly be challenged by other plausible interpretations, it strongly suggests that in pastoral therapy the broader institutional context may be a significant structural component impinging upon the therapeutic interaction. Such a position is analogous to the one taken in community psychiatry and especially by those interested in therapeutic communities.

Personal experience by the author in doing therapy in the homes of parishioners also has led to the conclusion that the context of pastoral therapy is important. In several situations pastoral calls led naturally into family therapy conducted in the home. When, after 10 sessions, appreciable changes were not occurring in the family system, the therapy was shifted to the church office and usually an immediate shift in the power structure of the family took place. The move to the church served to neutralize the power advantage of the dominant person in the family system. Admittedly, these cases were not individual pastoral therapy, but they highlight the importance of the constancy of structure unless a structural change is made as a therapeutic maneuver.

In discussing structural matters the pastoral therapist needs to define how she or he is going to handle missing sessions. Generally, it is best to indicate the person will pay for missing sessions unless the reason for absence is an absolute emergency. In this way the subtle acting out of feelings towards the therapist is discouraged and the therapy is inclined to move at a better pace. Missed sessions, besides being dealt with as a structural matter, need to be seen as resistance to the process of the therapy and as an effort by the person to slow down the therapy. Hence, it is more important for the therapist to insist on regular weekly visits rather than intermittent biweekly sessions. Again, vacations will inevitably occur, but they must be seen as a dilutant of the therapy and hence should be discouraged as much as possible at first.

The charging of fees is another structural matter. The tradition is most denominations is that pastors in their parish churches do not charge for short-term pastoral care. By short-term, as indicated earlier, anything up to four sessions is meant. However, there is a growing tendency in some local churches towards charging something for a non-contributing member of the church or a nonmember, where such a person seeks an inordinate amount of a pastor's time and can afford to pay. In such circumstances a person is charged on a sliding scale depending upon earning capacity. It has been the experience of pastoral therapists that while church members resist being charged large fees, they generally are not opposed to the principle of a fee system as such. What resistance does occur undoubtedly has multiple roots, but one major reason could be the inherent suspicion in protestantism that fees will represent a return to another form of indulgences.

Where pastors charge fees, they generally should not charge for the first session. By setting up pastoral therapy in this way, the therapist is able to handle many "one-session" situations on a pastoral care basis and still perform some of the broader functions of ministry where it is necessary. It also leaves persons free to come to the pastoral therapist to explore what is involved in therapy without having to be concerned about fees. A remarkable number of persons seeing a pastoral therapist once on a no-charge basis, see a therapist years later better prepared emotionally and financially for the effort involved in personality change.

A major reason for charging fees is obviously that fees help support the service given. But just as important a reason is that the charging of fees is generally in the best interest of the person seeking help. The following example comes from neurosurgery (Klink 1965).

> "Williamson, professor of neurological surgery, Kansas University Medical School, commenting on the recovery rate for surgery for ruptured disks has noted that in one neurosurgical clinic the cure rate for this operation in private patients is about 85%. For employees under Workman's Compensation laws liable not only for medical care, payment for time off and residence disability, the reported cure rate for the same operation by the same surgeon was only 35%. Comparable differences in cure rate have been reported in the Armed Forces during World War II and in the medical literature surveyed by Williamson."

The way a person seeking help responds to the structural matter of fees can be further diagnostic data. For example, a depressed person may state that the fee is too high and that she or he can't afford treatment because she or he is not worth spending anything on and does not deserve help anyway. The passive-aggressive person allows her or his bills to spiral because this assures that institutions and collectors will be interested in her or his welfare, with their badgering serving as a reassuring contact. The paranoid person may wonder if she or he is not being treated as someone special or as someone plotted against because of the fees charged. Among other diagnostic possibilities the obsessive-compulsive may see fees as sacrificial in nature. The hysterical woman may erotize the bill into a love note and carry it in her purse as "something personal" of the therapist that will be close to her. The narcissistic person often takes the bill, regardless of its appropriateness, as the signal to begin a fight. Then, there is the passive patient who insists on paying immediately to avoid any open conflict.

The concept of distance is also important for understanding the structural components of therapy. What seems to be emerging in the social science literature is the concept of "personal space," that is, that each person is surrounded by a series of concentric circles which represent different space boundaries. As W.H. Auden (1966) indicates:

"Some 30 inches from my nose
The frontier of my Person goes,
And all the untilled air between
Is private pagus or demesne.
Stranger, unless with bedroom eyes
I beckon you to fraternize,
Beware of rudely crossing it,
I have no gun, but I can spit."

The "30 inches" of Auden may not be literally accurate, but the notion of personal space is important.

Studies of persons in elevators further confirms the importance of personal space. As an elevator fills, persons take positions that maximize the distance between them. As the elevator becomes more crowded, the invasion of private territory is tolerated because it is only temporary, but even then, stiff posture, care not to touch or look at others and other aloof behaviors are used to offset the physically intimate distances and maintain emotional distance. In other words, physical distance generally is used as a major method of maintaining emotional distance, which is symbolic for the need to maintain (ego personal) boundaries.

Resistance to physical intimacy is understandable enough and seems to increase when the prospect of physical closeness will occur for an extended period of time. In comparison with a few minutes of temporary closeness in an elevator, a train ride of half an hour in close physical proximity places considerable strain on the other defenses against intimacy. Thus, at the Tokyo train station there are professional "packers" to push persons into crowded trains during the peak hours to overcome the natural resistance to physical closeness.

It is important for the pastor to realize that persons seeking help will be comfortable with different emotional and physical distances. For example, a schizophrenic person does not like closeness, expecially at the beginning of a relationship. Hanna Segel, (1963) once was the therapist of a schizophrenic patient who began analysis standing with his back to the therapist, a huge table between. Frankly, the author has listened to addresses to pastors where they were told that all interviews should be conducted without a table between. Like most rules it is generally but not always correct. Undoubtedly, the use of a table is a device for building distance into a relationship, but there are occasions when the person seeking help requires such distance. On the other hand, in most middle class churches the number of disturbed persons who come to the pastor needing physical distance built into the relationship will be small. Distance, then, is a structural component that must be varied until both the person and the pastor are comfortable, otherwise nothing meaningful will occur in the relationship.

On this matter of office furniture, (White 1953), a medical doctor did a study in which he removed his desk on alternate days to see the affect it had on his patients. He found that 55% of his patients were at ease when no desk was present, but 11% were more at ease when there was a desk. While this "ease" level was a subjective judgment by the doctor, the simple experiment does tend to confirm the conclusion that a desk and the resulting distancing is sometimes appropriate.

In psychotherapy the use of the couch can create distance, but it also fosters regression. Pastoral therapists generally do not use a couch, possibly as a symbol of professional boundaries with psychiatry. This in turn means that the pastoral therapist must learn to build into the structure of the therapeutic relationship other distancing devices. For example, face-to-face interviewing by pastoral therapists is generally not conducted with the person and pastor squarely confronting each other, but with chairs at a slight angle to facilitate looking away and keeping a reasonable level of comfort. However, the use of chairs rather than a couch does seem to lead to occasional requests for change in the seating arrangement by the person, and such requests need to be thoroughly investigated for their meaning. In one instance, a request by a person for the pastoral therapist to move his chair closer during the eighth session became a clue to the therapist of an increased level of trust and that the person was starting to accept the working alliance.

Karl Menninger in discussing the matter of distance, told of once receiving a letter requesting help. The letter itself was a distancing device, but the letter also contained a self-addressed envelope which suggested that the reader didn't think that she, the sender, was "worth a dime." Hence, the use of notes or letters can be a way for persons to keep distance in relationships. A phone call also can be a distancing device when compared with a personal appearance. A colleague once consulted about a client who would phone about two days after every third session. A careful review of the process notes revealed that in the session prior to each phone call there had been considerable "blocking" (inability to communicate associations) because of hostility to the therapist. Hence, the only way the client felt he could deal with the anger and continue the working alliance was to make a phone call, even though the call itself did not involve direct expressions of anger.

The form of address is yet another distancing device. It is suggested that all forms of address be kept formal using the terms Miss, Ms., Mr., or Mrs., unless the person is already known by a more informal name. Where the person is already on familiar terms, the therapist should explore carefully the issue of friendship to see whether this will undermine the chance of a significant working alliance. The pastoral therapist who finds it difficult not to use first names even where she or he didn't know the person previously, needs to look carefully at her or his own dynamic need for intimacy as a possible countertransference problem. Distancing generally enables more aggression to come out in the working relationship. If a pastor fears aggression she or he will often get "close to" the person as a way of avoiding the aggression being directed at her or him and sometimes go so far as to identify with the person. As Anna Freud (1966) explained, this is a defensive maneuver called "identification with the aggressor."

It is also important for the pastor to get some limits on the person's physical behavior that will be tolerated in therapy. The way this can be handled is by indicating what is permitted in the session as well as what is not (limits). For example, many therapists tell clients they "can do anything (positive) as long as they stay in the chair (negative)." This allows for a lot of anger and aggression to be expressed eventually by the person towards the therapist without a physical attack. It also allows for the person to express such exhibitionistic needs as taking off her or his clothes where this is necessary to resolve sexual conflict. Some pastoral therapists don't automatically set such behavioral limits except where they think they may be dealing with a severe acting-in behavior pattern. Such behavior is discussed in chapter 6. Others prefer to wait and see what develops in the relationship and only set behavioral limits when they think it is necessary.

One psychotherapist specifies one exception to doing anything while lying on the couch: he doesn't want the person to urinate. This is not because urinating is wrong, he explains to his patients, but because it makes him feel uncomfortable and because it is inconsiderate of other patients who also need to use the couch. Pastoral therapists will probably not work with persons as disturbed as this therapist does and hence may never run into the problem of a urinating client. Nevertheless, the concept of the therapist being able to monitor and verbalize her or his personal discomfort is important as a way of dealing with unusual or extreme acting-in problems in therapy, and in explaining the structural limitations set on a person's behavior. If the therapist is uncomfortable persons generally make little, if any, therapeutic progress.

In discussing structural matters with the person the pastoral therapist needs to tell her or him how the relationship may be terminated. Having just negotiated the therapeutic contract, such a structural manuever as discussing the "how" of termination may seem premature, but it is precisely because of the open length therapy that discussion of termination is necessary. If the process of therapy has more or less followed the procedures outlined in this book, the contract that is made after evaluation and interpretation is the third in a series of contracts. The first two contracts, it will be recalled are simple and closed. At the contact point the contract is to talk about the problem for one session. Toward the end of that session the contract is then made for another two or three sessions to evaluate the problem in more depth. There is, consequently, a certain security for the person to know that she or he still has control over the situation when a termination point is automatically built in. But once the contract is open and the termination point uncertain, it is important to have the person realize that she or he can still terminate at any time and also to know the procedures for this termination.

The person is told that termination is normally by mutual consent and that the number of session needed to terminate are generally proportionate to the length of therapy. However, either the person or the therapist has the right to request termination at any time, without the consent of the other, as long as enough notice is given for at least one complete session to discuss the reasons for the termination. This is meant to discourage premature termination as a means of acting out nonverbalized anger towards the therapist. It also enables a guilt-ridden person to terminate after going through a termination session and yet not have her or his guilt feelings reinforced because of the nature of the termination.

Room arrangements are another structural element. A quiet, comfortable, clean setting is so basic it may seem trite to mention this, but it can be easily overlooked by the pastoral therapist. A vacuum cleaner whining in an outer office, for example, can so distract a client that the session is unproductive, yet the client will politely say nothing. Church corridors will often magnify the noisey back slapping of well-intended fellowship and broadcast laughter and excited conversation like a loudspeaker. It is the pastoral therapist's responsiblity to stop such distraction even if it means leaving the office a few moments. Certainly, it is the pastoral therapists's responsibility to inquire whether the person is distracted if she or he thinks something in the setting is distracting the person, and then rectify the situation if this is possible. For example, it was the author's experience to have a gutter-cleaning contracting crew start erecting their ladders outside his office window in the middle of a session, so he immediately inquired whether this was distracting the client as much as it was distracting him. When the answer was affirmative he suggested they shift for the remainder of that session to a basement church school room, which, while cluttered, was quiet and private. This move led to a better working alliance because the person then had concrete evidence of the therapist's concern to do all he could to facilitate therapy.

In setting up an office the pastoral therapist is advised to have a comfortable chair for himself and both a hard chair and a comfortable chair, placed near each other, for her or his clients. These chairs are not only useful in situations where a couple come to see the pastoral therapist, but they often give a clue to who is being blamed for the marriage difficulty. For example, with one couple the wife quickly rushed to the hard chair, forcing the husband to take the softer one. In a later individual session the wife admitted that she thought her husband was to blame and had, in fact, sought to maniupulate him into therapy.

In individual work the author generally waves his hand vaguely towards the two chairs, and invites the person seeking help to take a seat. Those that select the hard chair are generally a lot more resistant to changing themselves and working in a therapeutic relationship despite their verbalizations. Also, in arranging a room the pastoral therapist should make sure that her or his chair is not so placed that it tends to block the person from getting to the door. Paranoid persons particularly don't like feeling trapped.

The matter of structure has been discussed in detail in this chapter because structuring is an unavoidable question if the pastoral therapist is to facilitate the working alliance. However, structuring issues are not just confined to explanations by the pastoral therapist as a part of contracting for therapy. Structural matters can occur at any stage of the therapeutic process. Sometimes, if the therapist has not dealt clearly with a structural matter the raising of such an issue by the person may result from consequential anxiety or misunderstanding. Such an issue may then be more an artifact introduced by the therapist than anything else. If questions about structure arise when the pastoral therapist has not clearly dealt with them, then she or he does not have any evidence of unconscious derivatives, even if they exist. Frequently questions of structure will involve internal conflicts reflective of childhood develop-ment which need to be resolved in the pastoral therapy. When a person in therapy acts to alter structure without discussing this with the therapist, this generally points to acting-in by the person. Hence, the more pains the therapist takes initially to explain structural questions, the more certain she or he can be that the person's attempt to manipulative structural change or to raise a structural question, points to an attempt to avoid remembering important repressed material. Hence, a person who comes to a session drunk needs to be dealt with structurally, that is, sent away and told to come to the next session sober, when the therapist has a chance to explore the reasons for the person getting drunk. Unfortunate-ly, it is too common a practice among pastors that they continue an "impossible" session with a drunk or semidrunk person, instead of dealing with this form of resistance to therapy via a structural maneuver, that is, by refusing to have the session.

Another way a client once changed the structural arrangements was to bring her spouse into the session unannounced when contracting had clearly been for an individual session with her. In this situation the spouse was asked to sit in the waiting room for a few moments while the pastoral therapist spent time with the person finding out why this acting-in was necessary. As a result the person decided she didn't want the therapist to talk with the spouse at all. If, during such a session, it becomes obvious that a session with the spouse would be advantageous to the client and the client wants this, the therapist can generally spend a few moments setting up a session especially for the spouse. The reader should understand that the therapist's reason for refusing to acquiesce automatically to a client's acting-in is because in forcing some discussion of the structural issue she or he can get at important repressed material which the person is resisting discussion of in therapy.

If there is a major difficulty for pastoral therapists, it occurs with acting-in. It is not easy for the well-liked pastor who uses the flexibility of the short-term pastoral care model, to detect acting-in. Nor has it been made easier when she or he has been trained with models that foster sloppiness under the guise of flexibility. Unless the therapist is prepared to give a great deal of attention to structural details, it is very clear the pastor should not attempt to conduct any kind of intensive, uncovering pastoral therapy.

The more dysfunctional the person being treated, the more crucial structure will be to the therapeutic outcome and the more sensitive the person generally is to structural components (Menninger 1963). This is illustrated by the work of Alfred Flarsheim (1972) who sometimes treats severely disturbed, borderline patients. These more extreme cases are discussed in the hopes that the pastoral therapist, who generally works with less disturbed persons, will nevertheless pay more attention to structural matters.

With such disturbed persons the primary purpose of structure is to provide environmental reliability and constancy (Winnicott 1966). This allows the person to use the "time frame" in various ways. Flarsheim describes one female client who, for 49 minutes, berated him because nothing was happening in the session. One minute before the end of the session she reported the fantasy of her mother being murdered in the house where she lived when she was four. By stating this fantasy one minute before the end of the session she was "saved by the bell" and relieved of pressure to reveal any more material than she was ready to do so at that time. Thus, she was able to maintain what precious little autonomy she still had but at the same time, uncover some material that needed to be revealed.

In another case the failure to provide a time frame resulted in a very clear negative communication from the client. The client reported a fantasy in which she carressed a woman's breast and the breast turned into flame. Suddenly the woman in the session screamed, "There is no end to it, it goes on forever." The therapist then noticed that the session had gone over by five minutes. Another dramatic use of the time frame was made by a 45-year-old surgeon who suffered from ulcerative colitis and had taken sedation every night for 10 years. After the initial sessions of dutifully reporting everything he ran out of material. He then went to sleep and was awakened at the end of the session. Each further session consisted of the patient coming in, falling into a deep sleep, and then waking up exactly 50 minutes later. This patient was able to use the time frame to experience in the therapeutic session what he was unable to experience outside of it!

Disturbed patients also notice many minute changes in structure. Flarsheim tells the story of his well-worn couch pillow. After years of pounding, the filling had moved from the middle and heaped itself around the edges. Feeling that his pillow was too shabby, he purchased a new one. But the reaction of most of his clients was surprising. Many of them became upset because of the failure of constancy in their environment. They poked and prodded at the new pillow, and in general, expressed their negative feelings. In one case, however, the woman who would normally cling to the couch because she feared it would tilt her to the floor said she experienced the new pillow in a very positive way. The discussion of the pillow led her to verbalize how much she depended upon the constancy of the therapeutic session. She felt the pillow symbolized how much little things were taken for granted. This led her to reflect that many things women do go unnoticed until they are not done and that this principle applies to most of the essential things of life. She went on to say that people don't thank floors and walls for existing, but they are a part of being able to function healthily and it was necessary to be able to take them for granted. Hence, reflects Flarsheim, the structure the therapist provides will not be noticed or overtly appreciated, but is the necessary foundation upon which any working alliance can take place. It is the therapist's task not to take for granted, but to monitor the structural components all the time. Pastoral therapists will do particularly well if they provide constancy of structure for psychotherapy.

Structure also provides therapists with, perhaps, the most effective way of dealing with manipulative or sociopathic personalities. Such persons need to experience an inability to manipulate structures as a way of testing their readiness for a working alliance. In one case (Jensen 1964) a 27-year-old single man who gave the appearance of being a very sincere and perplexed individual was seen for two interviews. His parents had been divorced soon after he was born so his grandparents had reared him. However, he found it extremely difficult to gain his freedom from a dominating grandmother. His father was in prison when the client came for therapy. His family doctor had seduced him into a homosexual relationship in his teen years and later he developed a homosexual relationship with one of his music professors in college. Just before seeking psychiatric help he had worked as a church organist in a small midwestern town but had come into conflict with the minister and resigned.

After the second interview the psychiatrist received a phone call from the client saying that he was in jail for writing a "no-fund" check. He wanted the psychiatrist to bail him out; however, the psychiatrist called an attorney who saw him in jail and found out that he had slipped out of the previous town owing a man $500. Two weeks later the man was released from jail and placed on probation. The attorney tried to get him a job, and he even covered two more "bad" checks. This time the person tried to get more appointments with the psychiatrist. The psychiatrist agreed to see the young man but decided, in view of the record, to make a structural move. He asked the person to pay for each session in cash. Within several weeks the man fled town. This case, although conducted by a psychiatrist, could have been handled by a pastoral therapist because it reflects a situation sometimes encountered in the parish.

In another case involving a pastoral therapist a structural matter became a critical feature at the beginning. A woman contacted the minister of counseling at a large Methodist Church by telephone from a small rural community 150 miles away. When the minister inquired about other possible resources closer to her home community, she admitted that they existed but said she didn't trust them because they were not "religious counselors." A date and time were set for a Saturday morning and confirmed by mail. However, the woman not only knocked on the minister's door a half hour before the session, but was surprised that he was seeing someone else at that time. She was asked to make herself comfortable in the waiting room area. Seen at the appointed hour, she eventually wanted the session to continue beyond the appointed time. It soon became apparent to the minister that her use of distance was meant to evoke sympathy from him so that she would be able to control the interview situation. He politely pointed out that the time was up and that he had someone else he had to see. He offered to see her the following week at the same time or refer her to a mental health clinic which was near her hometown. She accepted the appointment but canceled a few days later without explanation.

In this chapter it can be seen how crucial it is for the pastoral therapist to pay vigilant attention to structural matters. Some of the examples were of extreme situations but they were given to reinforce this point. Further, untrained pastors without adequate supervision generally get hopelessly enmeshed in structural entanglements if they attempt intensive, uncovering therapeutic work and this either means the person terminates the relationship (if they are fortunate to be well enough to do this), or else more serious damage occurs. Also apparent is the necessity for strict attention to structural matters by the pastor in pastoral care work. Moving casual contacts in church corridors to the quiet and comfort of an office can facilitate the helping process a lot. Setting up "one shot" appointments can be enough of a structuring maneuver to sift out those who really need the pastor's time and can be a signal to the person that the relationship is professional and not social. Professionalization of ministry that goes beyond rhetoric means taking structure more seriously than is generally done and using it more effectively than is typically the case.

5 : Working Alliance

Once a person has been evaluated, a contract reached, and structural arrangements made, the way is open for the therapy to move from the initial to the middle, or main, phase. Even though this phase is very much longer than the other two, the processes of the middle phase are more difficult to describe systematically. Like chess, therapy has circumscribed opening and closing moves but in between the possibilities are almost limitless.

Put simply, the middle phase consists of working to achieve the goals of the contract. In practice issues related to the structure of the therapeutic relationship, the working alliance, and distortions occur constantly and in a variety of ways. Any pastoral therapy process note for supervision on a middle phase session will reflect material on the unconscious struggle by the client to break therapeutic structure, undermine the working alliance, and distort what is happening to her or him. Hence, the issues of the middle phase are discussed chapters 4, 5, and 6 under the specific headings of therapeutic setting, working alliance, and distortion.

In this chapter, the focus is on the working alliance. This is because the working alliance is a key to determining whether pastoral therapy moves from the initial to middle phase. Just because a person comes to sessions does not mean that a working alliance is automatic. If it is going to develop, it generally takes time. Where it does not eventually develop, nothing by way of constructive change can occur, whether in pastoral therapy or in pastoral care. Although pastoral therapy and pastoral care will have different goals, unless an alliance is formed to work towards these goals, whatever they may be, ritualized stalemates will develop which lead to termination based on excuses (rationalizations).

In the previous chapter on structure, the part the therapist plays in forming a working alliance was discussed. The working alliance is the relatively nonneurotic rational rapport the client has with the pastoral therapist. It is formed between the client's reasonable ego (self) and the therapist's observing ego (self), and is constantly reinforced by the client's partial identification with the therapist's efforts at understanding (Greenson, 1965). This chapter focuses on specific contributions in the form of thoughts, feelings, dreams, and life-situation incidents that reflect the client's commitment to the alliance. Reporting such material, however, is easier said than done. When a person is asked to sit down, relax, and talk about whatever comes to mind, all kinds of resistances to producing thoughts are likely to occur. Hence, it will do so with the working alliance as the primary theme because the notion of resistance always raises the question of what is being resisted.

The concept of a working alliance was first introduced by Elizabeth Zetzel (1956), but it was not until nearly a decade later that Ralph Greenson (1968) made it more widely known to psychotherapists. While this term is proving to be useful for psychotherapists in general, it is extremely valuable for pastoral therapists as well. Out of the experience of supervising trainees in pastoral therapy, the author has noticed a frequent tendency for clergy to fall back on magical kinds of thinking, particularly to the idea that it is the power of the therapist's love (or personality) which changes persons. Despite the fact that this position conflicts with sound therapeutic training and practice, and is contrary to the agape (Nygren 1953) tradition in theology, a magical attitude towards therapy persists among clergy, especially among those without specialized training. To counteract this regressive tendency in clergy who are in training as therapists, the author, as a supervisor, found that by stressing the working alliance and giving it major attention in supervisory sessions, pastors generally learned faster and did better therapy.

Problems in establishing a viable working alliance will vary enormously, largely depending upon the personality of the client. A passive-dependent person, for example, tends to take the position that if she or he is patient and complying, the therapist will eventually reveal what the person should do in order to correct the presenting problem. This person places the therapist in the role of an authority figure whether the therapist seeks this or not, and, therefore, is resistant to the idea of a working alliance. Even where the therapist requests working material, this material is reported dutifully in order to please the therapist more than anything else. When no answers are forthcoming for a number of sessions, the passive-dependent person starts to get frustrated with the therapist so that unless she or he can get the person to see that her or his perception of therapy is inaccurate, the person generally terminates the relationship after a number of sessions feeling that "therapy" is a waste of time. And, of course, the therapy is a waste of time unless a working alliance is formed. To this extent, the passive-dependent feelings are accurate. The pity is that such people think they have been "in therapy" when, in fact, the therapy never reached middle phase.

As indicated earlier, the author's approach to the working alliance is to explain to the client that the therapist's major responsibility is for structuring the relationship, while the client's is to provide the material of the sessions in the form of thoughts, feelings, incidents, slips of the tongue, and dreams. As Sullivan indicates, this will not automatically or immediately happen. When the person spontaneously reports material for the first time, especially thoughts or feelings that have suddenly come to mind during the session, it is pointed out that this is the kind of material being sought. In other words, an example is better than telling the client theory, and what better example can one use than one from a client's own behavior. When that example occurs, it should be reinforced immediately.

When a therapist requests dream material, the person often replies that she or he doesn't dream. One of the most effective ways of handling this is to point out briefly the results of the rapid eye movement (REM) studies. During sleep, there are, at regular intervals, periods of a few minutes in which the sleeper's eyes move rapidly beneath the eyelids. If subjects of the studies were awakened during these REM periods, they were able to relate the dreams they had just experienced. Many of these subjects were persons who, at first, claimed they did not dream. The real point, then, is not that a person doesn't dream, but that she or he doesn't remember dreams. In explaining this to the client, it needs to be said that not remembering dreams is understandable enough when such remembering didn't serve any worthwhile purpose. It can then be posed that a task during this phase of the therapy is for the person to train herself or himself to remember more of her or his dreams. Again, in making this explanation the therapist has the effect of stressing therapy as work and not magic. In the author's experience, some dreams generally are reported a session or two after this explanation is made to the client.

Even though dreams are a part of the biblical and religious tradition, it has not been the custom for clergy to encourage a parishioner to report dreams when she or he seeks help. This makes sense if the pastoral relationship is for one or two sessions where the magical expectations are met with loving reassurance and the goal of the interaction is not personality change. All experienced clergy can point to many such situations where the mystique of the role (office) of the clergyman was useful in strengthening a parishioner through a temporary stress situation. However, it also needs to be recognized that even in such a short-term relationship where dreams are not encouraged, dreams will sometimes get reported. Hence, because the handling of dreams is of some importance to all clergy, whether a pastoral specialist or not, this matter will be given further attention.

One of the most common assumptions made is that there are certain meanings to dreams, universal symbols which, when dreamed, always mean the same thing. Under this view, when one wants a dream interpreted one goes to an expert (authority figure) who can explain what the dream means because she or he holds the secrets to dream interpretation. To the extent that this idea is prevalent, psychotherapy will be open to the charge in Christian theological circles of being a modern gnostic movement, and, therefore, suspect. However, trained psychotherapists do not approach dream work as experts in universal symbols, even though some symbols seem to have common meanings. An approach to dream work can be illustrated by what took place at a party where a woman, for curiosity, presented the author with a dream. In this situation the person's position was "demythologized" by pointing out that dreams tend to lack universal meaning and that if the author gave an off-the-cuff interpretation, it would probably be wrong. This statement pleasantly surprised the person.

One of the ways to increase the reliability of dream interpretation is to work within the context of a continuing personal relationship. The value of dream interpretation increases when reported material over a long period of time becomes the context of the interpretation. In this way dreams are seen as one element in the general work of therapy, and the usefulness of dreams is increased when their meaning evolves out of the general flow of therapeutic material itself. Thus, other types of data and a longitudinal approach serve as "cross bearings" on any interpretation that may be given for a dream.

This position only goes half way. It still leaves the therapist as the expert, a more careful, systematic, skillful expert, but an expert, nevertheless. The best interpretations not only make more sense when seen in terms of the general process of the therapy, but also when they come from the person's own struggles with dreams. Thus, a suitable response of the therapist to the reporting of a dream is something like, "What comes to your mind in connection with the dream?" In other words, dreams in therapy become the starting point for associative work by the client, not a cue for the expert to give an association-stifling answer. What a person associates with a dream is considered more valuable than the dream itself.

The importance of the context of an intense relationship and of associative material to dream interpretation is illustrated by the dream of a woman, a single parent in her mid 30s, after she had been in therapy for approximately 200 sessions. In the first part of the dream she watched the TV set where her boyfriend was playing football. The scene changed to a large, tastefully furnished living room where there were about a dozen affluent, white, late-middle-aged ladies dressed in their furs and jewels. When the client walked into the room they invited her to sit down. The picture then changed to a swimming pool where the client and her two children dived and frolicked. However, the swimming pool turned into a water-race along which she and her children were swept until they fell down a large waterfall into a deep pool. After surviving the fall they tried to swim back towards the waterfall but could not make progress against the current. The client awakened from the dream fearful and perspiring.

There are many possible interpretations to this dream with its many elements. One student, for example, suggested that the boyfriend would, maybe, make money and be a means of getting her into the class represented by the "fat cats." On the other hand, she was afraid of getting into this kind of relationship as represented by her jumping into the pool and being swept away. Another student suggested that the pool and children were a symbol of the sexual relationship with the boyfriend of which the ladies disapproved, and the fall and fear of drowning, symbols of punishment and guilt feelings. All of this was speculative, of course. However, a knowledge of the case and the associations of the person herself made it very clear that the boyfriend and matrons represented controlling (narcissistic objects) relationships (narcissistic objects) to which she had (masochistically) surrendered herself in her past. Further, mature independence in which she would take care of the children and raise them herself, was a dangerous choice; but now she had chosen this path there was really no turning back. However, there is also fear that she and the children will not make it and will die. The dream had followed a session where she realized that no knight in shining armor would rescue her and that unless she took care of herself and her children, no one else would. She, herself was able to make this interpretation of the dream, remarking, "The dream didn't make us (she included the therapist) aware of anything we didn't already know, but it feels good to get confirmation and agreement from the deeper recesses of the mind." A lot of dreams serve this function.

Dream interpretation is but another example of the fact that therapy is work for the client as well as the therapist. Like any kind of work, the work of therapy gets resisted. One biblical term for resistance is "hardening of the heart," but the type of resistance more likely to emerge in response to the need to produce material in the session is some form of avoidance of "game playing." The author has seen dozens of cases where the game playing goes on for about eight or 10 sessions until the person terminates the "therapy." Obviously, allowing the game playing to continue without dealing with it in some way is detrimental to the therapy, yet it needs to be understood that resistance, as such, is not a bad thing. It is not only that resistance should be expected and tolerated for a while, but that resistance is a good prognostic sign if it can be slowly resolved. Some resistance is good because it points to (ego) strength in the personality which is eventually going to be necessary for changing the personality structure as agreed in the contract. Hence, resistance ultimately enables a successful outcome for the therapy.

One type of resistance is an absence of associations. The person comes in and says that she or he has nothing to talk about; that nothing happened of importance during the week and that she or he had no dreams to report. In doing this the person has unconsciously resorted to tossing the glove into the center of the ring. If the challenge is accepted by the therapist then the "battle of the toilet" begins all over again. Obsessive-compulsive personalities are particularly adept at provoking these competitive forms of resistance. Essentially, they have the compulsion to re-enact an original battle of wills over demand for training by an authority figure. Toilet training is considered to be the classic area where the original battle took place, but experience has shown that wherever the infant had unempathic demands placed on her or him, the struggle of wills could emerge over such matters as feeding habits, toilet training, dressing, or learning language. Essentially, the issue is being forced to produce.

In the development of a healthy child these requests by the loved parent for modified behavior are generally responded to by the child doing what is asked as a favor. For example, when the child first defecates in the potty it is generally an accident. However, if the parents make a fuss over such behavior and praise the child for the stool produced, she or he thereby learns to produce stools in the potty as gifts, and as an act of love for the parents who are loving and kind to her or him. The child does not do this because she or he needs to learn this behavior eventually to be a better adult, or for any rational reason at all. But where force is used in the socializing of a child, ambivalent feelings remain which get regenerated when the therapist, in innocence, asks the person to produce material for the session. Where resistance occurs to the working alliance in such a person the therapist needs to be patient for a while and allow some trust to develop so that the person has a chance eventually to offer the material as something for which she or he receives praise.

At the beginning of the middle phase, when a person indicates she or he has nothing to talk about, the therapist has an opportunity to show by behavior she or he has no intentions of forcing the person to produce. The author's response is to say, "In that case why don't you sit back, relax, and tell me what comes into your mind." Sometimes, after a few moments, this will be enough for the person to start communicating her or his thoughts and feelings. Others, however, will lapse into silence and possibly use this silence to set up a potential competitive battle. To play this game the therapist must be determined that at all costs she or he will remain silent until the person speaks. During training a friend of the author found himself in one of these initial silences for about half of one session and nearly all of the next session until he eventually decided that this was not going to achieve anything. If such a competitive silence seems to be developing, there is every good reason for the therapist to break the silence and avoid a clash of wills. Silences broken by the therapist because she or he feels threatened by them are another matter. In this case the feelings (countertransference) of the therapist involved need to be carefully explored in a supervisory session. In breaking the silence the pastoral therapist needs to have the attitude that she or he wants to explore the reason for it. As a first move she or he could ask if the person is aware of any reason for the silence which has occurred. If the person is in touch with the reason, the discussion which results can be an important step towards the kind of openness and trust necessary for a good working alliance. If the person is not consciously aware of the reason for the silence, raising the question enables the therapist to show that she or he is more interested in understanding the situation than pressuring the person to produce.

When the person is unaware of any possible reason for the silence, but seems interested in making the reason for the silence the work focus, the pastoral therapist could gently explore a few possibilities. The therapist could ask, for example, if the person is feeling a little insecure about the treatment. Or the therapist could explore with the person whether there is anything that makes her or him feel anxious about the therapist. This kind of exploration, if done with tentativeness and in spirit of initial inquiry, again shifts the dynamics of the interaction away from a competitive one to a cooperative working alliance, whether any reasons for the resistance are discovered or not. Such moves on the part of the therapist will also help to build trust. To the extent the person trusts the therapist, she or he will find it easier to reveal herself or himself and bring material into the sessions necessary for a successful outcome. If all of the above moves do not work, then it is necessary to explore why it is difficult for the person to trust the therapist. Again, the person may not know, but at least the therapy gets focused on the key issue as soon as possible.

Another common defense against the working alliance is the persistent discussion of symptoms. While filling the session with verbiage is generally accepted for a little while, the therapist eventually needs to get the person away from giving a defensive monologue. One possible maneuver is to suggest that all of the matters she or he has been talking about point to some common theme, and then wonder what this could be. Of course, the person generally doesn't consciously know, but at least the raising of the question takes the focus away from the symptoms. If trying to move the session away from extraneous details and towards a focus fails, then another tactic could be to place the attention on the process of the therapy rather than the content, that is, it can be reflected that the person seems to have difficulty in talking about personal matters. If this doesn't lead to some meaningful interaction, then it may be necessary to explore with the person if she or he has any doubts about the usefulness of the treatment.

Yet another defense against the working alliance is intellectualization. If the person uses psychological or theological language or any technical word, it pays the pastoral therapist to ask what is meant by these words in simple terms. In this way the barriers implicit in the use of technical terminology are avoided until, with the reduction of anxiety, the use of technical language is abandoned. A different version of this tactic is when the person tries to get the therapist into an intellectual discussion of something. On these occasions the pastoral therapist needs to gently suggest that this kind of discussion is not the purpose of the session and that it would be better accomplished over a cup of coffee or in a "bull session." If, however, the person has a compulsive need to find an explanation for everything it is possible to start interrupting the monologue with something like, "Yes, I see, but the main point you are making seems to be. . . ." On the other hand some intellectualizers are generalists in that they describe many incidents rather superficially. With such persons it is possible to start a working alliance by stopping the conversation after a while and asking for details of what happened in the incident. In other words, the object is to move the person from a string of interpretations to giving concrete data on which the pastoral therapist can bring her or his own judgment to bear. In addition to asking for the data behind the general interpretations, it is also extremely important to ask how the person personally felt about something. After some time this kind of selective responding helps produce a viable working alliance, the major goal of the initial part of the middle phase.

A further example of resistance to the working alliance is the hysteric. Joseph Coltrera and Nathanial Ross (1967) say, "The affective storms of the hysterical character form a major resistance." What generally happens is that the hysterical person comes into a session all upset about something, the only question being the degree of the upset. Often, if allowed, a session will become a complaining binge. Again, this pattern can be allowed for a session or two but eventually the person can be interrupted by asking her or him to relate what happened. In other words, asking for facts gets away from the swamp of feelings and prepares the way for some summarizing statements further in the session or in a later session. Helping the hysteric gain a cognitive map of what is happening gives her or him an intellectual structure with which to understand the events that have occurred. This is another variation of the therapeutic adage in chapter 4 that structure (this time, cognitive) binds anxiety. With the lowering of anxiety there is far less attempt at control by the person and the way is then open for further development of the working alliance.

Often the tactics mentioned as ways of facilitating the working alliance work, but sometimes no matter what the pastoral therapist does, the resistance to a working alliance remains. Ultimately, the person has a right to her or his silence, confusion, or verbiage. Because the pastoral therapist is not a manipulator, she or he may have to allow the person to resist until she or he accepts a working alliance. For some persons whose resistance is light, the facilitating moves of the pastoral therapist can help save time and move the process of the therapy along. On the other hand, strongly resisting persons may be inclined to see such facilitation as pressure to produce and hence may resist all the more. Rather than help move the therapy along, "facilitating" responses can delay it longer.

Acting-out and its "cousin" acting-in are still further ways a person may choose to resist treatment. By acting-out it is meant a person expresses her or his feelings through some action rather than remembering or verbalizing the feelings. For example, a married woman who had been in therapy for 15 sessions was unable to express her deep-seated anger about her husband, and, more importantly, about her father. As an impasse developed in the therapy, she was unable to express any of her anger and frustration towards the pastoral therapist. One weekend, she compulsively journeyed several hundred miles to an old male friend and had a weekend "affair" with him. The pastoral therapist not only suggested that the friend had been a substitute for him, but also suggested that she had resorted to this behavior as a displaced and symbolic form of sexual resistance. At first she denied the resistance, but later in the session suddenly remembered just how angry she was at her father who had never accepted her as a person in her own right, but had kept her infantilized to meet one of his own needs. This affair was a form of acting which resisted the remembering, but it was action outside the therapeutic sessions. It is only available as material in the session if the person mentions it. When acting-out is reported, the pastoral therapist's focusing on the acting-out is meant to eventually uncover the memory that lies behind this behavior.

Chessick (1974) thinks that a therapist must always be alert to the possibility of acting-out behavior. He thinks it is a "particularly pernicious form of resistance because it can break up the therapy entirely, if it is not correctly recognized and dealt with." The author is in complete agreement with Chessick about this, and has discovered that pastoral therapists often have a difficult time recognizing acting-out before it leads to the breakup of the therapy. One classic form of acting-out has been called "flight into health," which is where the acting-out is rationalized into the idea that the person is cured.

Acting-in could be, in one sense, considered as a variation of acting-out. Like acting-out, acting-in depends upon action as a means of blocking but also indirectly expressing a memory. The acting occurs in the therapy session, not outside it. Thus if the "out" and the "in" take the therapy session as a reference point, strictly speaking the terms acting-out and acting-in describe behavior of persons who are undergoing psychotherapy only. They are seen as forms of resistance to memories which the stimulation of therapy is bringing back into consciousness. In more popular usage most forms of behavior which express thoughts or feelings through action are wrongly referred to as acting-out even though the person may be consciously aware of what these may be, but prefers to act them anyway.

One form of acting-in is the bringing of gifts to the pastoral therapist. For example, one pastoral therapy supervisee kept reporting a stalemate until, it was accidently discovered, that the client always came into the therapy session with a cup of coffee for both the therapist and herself. When this was pointed out to the supervisee as resistance through acting-in, he got in touch with his feelings that the person fantasied the relationship as a social or sexual one in which she received gratification rather than worked at changing herself. When the supervisee interpreted this to the person in the next therapy session she started to produce material in the form of thoughts, feelings, and dreams and the therapy started to progress again.

Meyer Zeligs (1957), in describing the term acting-in, saw it as really a "middle point" in a continuum of acting-out without remembering and verbalizing, and verbalizing and remembering without acting at the other end. In the sense that the behavior is accessible to the therapist without the need of the person to report it, acting-in is more preferable than acting-out. On the other hand, having to deal with it directly in the session can make the acting-in behavior a lot more critical. For example, obvious forms of acting-in behavior are the missing of sessions and being late for them. These behaviors have to be looked at if any significant therapy is to take place. Allowing missing sessions or lateness to go on without investigation generally means the therapist is sanctioning a relational homeostasis where psychic energy necessary for a change is constantly being drained off and not made available as typical therapeutic material. Hence, the therapeutic move is to see acting-out and acting-in behavior as data for the therapy and help the person explore the meaning of that behavior.

In discussing acting-in Chessick (1974) describes the behavior of a 30-year-old nurse. At first she tried to manipulate a premature termination of therapy by saying she was being cheated. She said she had talked this over with her doctors and they supported her objections to the therapy. When this didn't work, she said she had to terminate because she couldn't afford the therapy. When the therapist was able to show this was not accurate, she tried to get jobs so that she would not have time for the therapy. Acting-in behavior generally involves the structure of the therapy itself in one way or another. Hence, the clearer and firmer the therapist has been in establishing the structure of the therapy, the easier it is to detect and deal with acting-in behavior. This does not mean that the behavior has to be prevented, but it makes it easier to get the person to cooperate in looking at the meaning behind the behavior. For example, if a person says there is an emergency and wants to use the telephone during the session, this can be allowed, but then this act becomes data for the session.

Where structural matters have not been clearly established at the beginning of the therapy, acting-in behavior is not only more difficult to detect, but even more difficult to interpret to the person because of the defensive denial that will take place in the session. Pastors consistently have difficulty in setting up clear and firm structures in any serious attempts at changing persons through "counseling." This seems to be because a pastor generally likes to see herself or himself as a good person who offers care and healing, and it doesn't seem like she or he is caring if she or he is firm and professional. As long as the pastor keeps to the caring role and sees persons on an occasional one-session basis, her or his ministry can be helpful. It is when the pastor tries to mix pastoral care and pastoral therapy, that so many of the problems arising in pastoral therapy occur, unless the pastor has training to counter the tendency in ministry to "mother" clients.

An even further difficulty comes about because many trained pastoral therapy specialists have modes of therapy that pay only token attention to both evaluation and structure. Hence, because acting-in is generally not seen as significant, many of the persons whose major formal dynamic material is presented as subtle acting-in behavior, get either locked into interminable, ritualistic sessions with such therapists, or, more likely, withdraw from the therapy after a few sessions.

If such nonstructured therapy just evolved into "therapy interminable," there probably would be little damage done. Unfortunately, those sessions can involve more than a ritualistic stalemate. The need to care for or feed the person can foster gross acting-out. The need for the therapist to mother persons has to be seen as an example of the therapist's own acting-in behavior which, in turn, reflects the therapist's countertransference feelings.

A study that clearly shows the way in which a therapist's acting-in leads to client acting-out behavior was reported from the Menninger Foundation (Cancro 1968). It was done on "elopements," which consisted of patients leaving the Menninger Hospital without permission. These elopements were seen as basically hysterical symptoms where a conflict is acted out. There were more women than men elopements, the mean age of patients who eloped was in the early 20s, and there was an infectious quality of the elopements. Seeing these elopements as hysterical acting-out behavior was useful because it led to the immediate hypothesis that the behavior was a defense against a threatening aspect of the doctor-patient relationship. This hypothesis, in turn, suggested that countertransference in the form of the therapist's acting-in behavior motivated the elopements. The specific problem was the doctor's excessive involvement with the patient.

This conclusion was confirmed most dramatically by two nursing supervisors who made the observation that elopements are frequently preceded by written orders from the doctor which state, "Refer all the patient's requests to me." They also stated that when the doctor has difficulty in "sharing" a particular patient with the rest of the therapeutic team, the patient is very likely to elope. All of this was illustrated by an elopement of a male patient which was followed in few minutes by the elopement of his hospital girlfriend. She sought to find him and bring him back to the hospital. If he refused to return, her conscious fantasy was that she would bring him to the hospital doctor's home. Subsequent psychotherapy revealed that the boyfriend's sudden leaving the hospital left her at the mercy of her sexual feelings so she wanted to deliver him to the doctor as a magical amulet to protect her from these feelings. Thus, when a therapist can't respect the client's need for distance, she or he is acting in the therapy one of her or his own needs and inviting acting-out by the client.

Another example of acting-in behavior also comes from the Menninger Hospital in an account of "staying-in-bed" behavior by three patients (Sheafer 1968). Staying in bed, which was obviously a resistance to treatment, consisted of a repeated failure to arise in time for the first activity of the day after several reminders from nursing personnel. The patients studied had, despite superior intelligence, severally disappointed their parents by failing in school. Thus, staying in bed was an act of hostility and rebelliousness towards their parents and parental surrogates, particularly the doctors and nurses. Also, by staying in bed they were able to act out their dependency needs and make the staff aware of what helpless infants they were. And, as mentioned, by staying in bed they kept the therapists at a distance and hence resisted the therapy.

The study of elopements from the Menninger Hospital is a reminder of the way resistance to the working alliance can be fostered by the therapist. Levinson (1962) reminds that just as drugs can have an iatrogenic (the treatment causes a worse illness) effect, so any intervention, whether it be on an individual or a social system level, can be iatrogenic. One way this effect manifests itself with pastoral therapists is with premature interpretations or ones that are seen as unacceptable, such as an interpretation that the person is angry, when that person comes from a family or church where it was "un-Christian" to feel or express anger. Thus, an interpretation that cuts across the beliefs of the person's reference group at an early stage in the therapy can produce considerable resistance which can prolong the therapy unnecessarily, if not lead to a premature termination. Sexual interpretations, especially in the early part of the middle phase, can also build up a great deal of resistance. It is, unfortunately, true that many pastors, still living under a popularized and distorted view of Freud, think that therapy basically means dealing with sex. So they wrongly think that the sooner they get to the sex material the sooner the person will be helped. While no area of a person's life can be allowed to be taboo if a person enters the therapeutic alliance, one of the basic rules is that nothing should be sexualized that can be dealt with nonsexually to avoid building up any unnecessary resistance. Hence, sexual matters should be left until well into the middle phase, unless, of course, the person herself or himself raises them earlier.

While resistance occurs constantly in the therapeutic relationship, it generally reaches one of its peaks in the early part of therapy. It is often experienced that, after an initial period of strong resistance, a shift towards less resistance will occur. One of the ways this shift has been noticed is in the fact that the person will ask, "How are you?", at the opening of the session. This apparently innocent, ritualistic greeting often hides a deeper meaning, which, in the context of the therapy, seems to say, "You are important to me, I am commencing to trust you." Students without any experience in attempting pastoral therapy sometimes challenge this interpretation, feeling there are insufficient grounds to make it. They say the person is just being polite and giving the social amenity of a greeting. To this criticism there is the question of why there is this specific greeting and not some other, and why it often occurs after two or three months. However, the most telling argument comes from the behavior that generally follows that initial greeting. Consistently the author has found a shift after such a greeting to a more willing participation in the working alliance.

As just indicated, resistances will occur in the therapy even after the development of a solid working alliance. An example of this is where a number of productive sessions are followed by one that is full of resistances and seems unproductive. When this occurs, one way of dealing with it is to assure the person that plateaus will occur in the therapy and, therefore, she or he should not be unduly troubled by them. Another procedure which has proved invaluable is to go back over the notes of the previous productive session looking for something that has not been adequately dealt with. If some issue is found, raising it at the following session often brings forth a torrent of repressed associations.

A common problem for supervisees in pastoral therapy is the resistance of the person to the therapist's interpretation. Beginning therapists can be premature or wild in their interpretations and so provoke the resistances that occur. What tends to trouble most beginning supervisees is that when data have accumulated on the case so that the interpretation is sound, the resistance is often the greatest. In other words, resistance when the therapist is wrong or possibly wrong is understandable, but resistance when the evidence points to the therapist being right, so thinks the supervisee, is "unreasonable." But that is the point of therapy! It is the "unreasonableness" of the person which has led her or him into therapy in the first place. The ferocious resistance that a sound therapeutic interpretation sometimes fosters comes because the interpretation has penetrated the repression, is recognized as having some validity, and so is vehemently denied. Despite the denial, the seeds of change are sown by sound interpretations; the resistance should be accepted by the therapist without getting upset. Another reason why a sound interpretation is resisted, even when its truth is privately acknowledged by the person, is that the person feels she or he must resist on principle or else be in danger of losing her or his autonomy. Accepting interpretations looks too much like conforming to an authority figure. However, the better the working alliance, the more these dynamics will be minimized.

Freud (1909) himself discusses this question of the client rejecting interpretations. As he indicates, one of his clients "admitted that all of this (interpretation) sounded quite plausible, but he was naturally not in the very least convinced by it." Then, as Freud goes on, he clearly enunciates the major theme of this chapter. He says, "It is never the aim of discussions like this to create conviction. *They are only intended to bring the repressed complex into consciousness,* to set the conflict going in the field of conscious mental capacity, and to facilitate the emergence of fresh material from the unconscious. A sense of conviction is only attained after the patient has himself worked over the reclaimed material, and so long as he is not fully convinced, the subject must be considered as unexhausted." In other words, even interpretations serve to produce material for therapy sessions in addition to dreams, thoughts, incidents, and acting behavior.

As mentioned earlier in the chapter, sometimes a person comes in and says she or he doesn't know what to talk about, and suggestions were made as to how to deal with this resistance to the establishment of a working alliance. On these occasions the author may allow some silence, which enables the person to relax and not feel pushed, and then the thoughts start flowing. However, some years ago, after being confronted by a very resistant person who had "nothing to say," the author realized that the session had turned out to be one of his most productive. After that similar situations were observed and found that they, too, were usually most productive even though the person started out by saying she or he "had nothing to say." Hence, based on past experience the author now responds to the person by saying, "I have learned that sessions starting out with persons having nothing to say have turned out to be some of the best." Saying this to the person seems to be enough to trigger contribution of a lot of significant material which the person had resisted reaching consciousness.

In stressing resistances to the working alliance, this chapter has touched on issues sometimes discussed under the term transference, which the classical therapist uses to describe resistances to the working alliance, and, in fact, everything that happens to the relationship. By transference the author means distortions to the relationship with the therapist because of past relationships with parents or parental surrogates. Other therapists, however, have suggested that transference may be better seen as a special form of resistance. Whatever the theoretical merits of each case may be, the author has found it advantageous to teach the concept of resistance to the working alliance to pastoral therapists without stressing the transference elements. Clergy often come for training with misperceptions about transference and these distortions create resistance to learning about the process of therapy. What is perhaps more important, in practice the author has found supervisees who have been encouraged to focus on the working alliance at the beginning of the middle phase have less sticky early transference problems with their clients.

While the subject of transference will be looked at in detail in the next chapter, it is pertinent to say here that much that gets explained by beginning therapists as transference may be iatrogenic material, that is, reactions of the client to the neophyte's or ill-trained therapist's bungling efforts to establish a working alliance. Even though some of this material probably would have emerged anyway, the emergence of it in strength and at such an early stage makes it infinitely more difficult to handle or resolve. In stressing the question of iatrogenic effects the author is suggesting there is a difference between lack of skill in the beginning pastoral therapist and resistance of the pastoral therapist to the working alliance because of her or his own unresolved countertransference feelings, that is, the transferences she or he brings to the relationship. For some neophytes the experience of a number of cases in which the focus is on the establishing of a working alliance enables them to quickly gain some of skills, whereas other neophyte pastoral therapists always have to struggle to establish a working alliance because of their own countertransferences. In the case of countertransference problems interfering with the establishment of a working alliance, the beginning therapist needs to get further therapy for herself or himself before she or he can perform successfully.

Likewise, some persons coming into therapy may resist the working alliance no matter how skillful the pastoral therapist. The issue in supervision, however, is whether the inability to establish the working alliance is because of newness, countertransference, or transference. With the pastoral therapist on her or his first case, it would probably be all three. If the newness can be ruled out, then a clue to the issue of whether the resistance to the working alliance is due primarily to the person's transference or the therapist's countertransference may be in the therapist's relationship with the supervisor. If the supervisor is finding it hard to get a working alliance going with the supervisee (with different goals than in the therapy relationship), then it is most likely that the supervisee is unable to establish a working alliance with the person. If the supervisor-supervisee working alliance is good, then the problems with the working alliance in the therapy relationship are most likely a form of transference, especially if the therapist has worked at any obvious resistances and still failed to establish an alliance after a reasonable period of time.

Behind the notion of dealing first with resistances to a working alliance is an assumption that needs verbalizing. The pastoral therapist works towards this goal, not just because she or he knows the therapeutic value of the working alliance, but because of a belief that there are repressed maturational forces within the person's personality which, when tapped, can do the person infinitely more good than anything or anyone including the therapist can do. This belief in the power of maturational forces can be intellectual, but generally gets affirmed during the pastoral therapist's own therapy. Once this has occurred in the therapist's experience it gets reinforced with every successful case thereafter, and is communicated nonverbally as quiet confidence.

Having stressed the idea of working at the alliance so heavily in this chapter, it seems appropriate to say a word about play. By play the negative connotation attached to game playing as used earlier and made famous by Berne (1966) is not meant, but the original notion of game as trial and error. Once the working alliance is established the person is really free to explore playfully many things in the therapeutic relationship, where there are no major penalties for the thoughts, feelings, and dreams discussed. As long as major decisions and the behavior associated with them are discussed first with the therapist who can warn against destructive consequences, perhaps stimulated by the play of therapy, the person can discover that the working alliance is a very freeing and unique experience.

6 : Distortion

In a classical textbook on psychotherapy, this chapter would be titled "transference," a term introduced by Freud and one that has attracted more attention in therapeutic writings than any other. The term distortion, as used here, however, is derived from Sullivan's (1954) concept of parataxic distortion which describes the process that interferes with the realistic factors of a healthy relationship. Distortion, as a concept, is used because it enables one to look at transference in its broadest sense. Besides discussing repetition compulsion, transference, and countertransference as forms of distortion, this chapter shall also cover such matters as transference-like phenomena and externalization.

In training pastors and pastoral therapy specialists, the author has discovered that an emphasis on the concept of repetition compulsion early in the training rather than on transference leads to better therapeutic results. Simplified, repetition compulsion is where a person finds herself or himself repeating the same mistake or painful experience in many, if not all of her or his personal relationships. Once a person moves into the middle phase of therapy, the neophyte pastoral therapist needs to give attention to material on repetition compulsion as well as material which affects the working alliance and structure. Naturally, it would be convenient if persons first gave material that only reflected problems of the working alliance or structure and, once these were resolved, gave material related to repetition compulsion. In practice, of course, it never happens this way. Matters that reflect the working alliance, structure, and repetition compulsion get presented together, in the same session, and are, in fact, linked dynamically. Out of a need to compulsively repeat a relationship pattern from the past a person will bring some form of resistance to the working alliance often as a breaking of structure.

This intermixing of the material of repetition compulsion, structure, and working alliance can be confusing to the beginning pastoral therapist. It seems to help such a therapist to know that while repetition compulsion, structure, and working alliance are often intertwined, they present themselves as the major foci for the therapist during the initial part of the middle phase. As a general rule, however, the therapist should select material in such a way that structural issues come first, then the needs of the working alliance take precedence over helping the person understand the extent of the repetition compulsion. For example, a female with a hysterical personality, after being evaluated, and after contracting for therapy during the fourth session, came 10 minutes late for the eighth session with a flimsy excuse. The therapist decided not to raise the question of her lateness even though he saw the lateness as acting-in behavior that reflected her resistance to the working alliance. During supervision the therapist indicated he had not focused on the lateness because he felt that the person was not sufficiently anchored in a working alliance with him. Instead, he was able to discuss with her her fear of dependency which was the content of the material she had presented during the session. The therapist realized that the lateness was another way the person expressed her fear of dependence, but wanted to keep to the level of the more obvious content as a way of avoiding anything that would disturb the growing working alliance.

The purpose in mentioning this specific piece of behavior and the decision of the therapist is not to suggest that there is a "correct" way to conduct therapy. Rather, it illustrates the way the working alliance was used as the basis for a decision not to raise the structural issue of the lateness of the person. Someone else might have been able to interpret the behavior during the latter part of the session as another expression of the person's fear of dependence, and not only "got away with it," but actually strengthened the working alliance. However, even if this maneuver by another therapist had successfully taken place, the basis of the decision would have been an attempt to strengthen the working alliance, just as with the decision of the first pastoral therapist. It will be seen from this that therapists will often do different things with the same material. When there is a sound basis for what is being done, and the therapist is comfortable with it, the results are generally constructive.

The lateness of this person for the eighth session warrants further attention. If the person was also late for the next session or sessions, the therapist could raise the structural question of the meaning of this behavior with less risk to the working alliance than with the evidence of just one late session. It is, obviously, more difficult to believe that late behavior for several successive sessions is accidental or random. The therapist can suggest that the behavior of being late is another way of expressing the person's fear of dependency, and in so doing makes the person aware of the congruence between the person's behavior and her verbalized thoughts and feelings about dependency. This working for congruence between the three faculties of cognition (thoughts), affection (feelings), and conation (action) is an important task during therapy, but it is always secondary to the needs of the working alliance and structural matters in the initial part of the middle phase. That is, if pressing for congruence could endanger the working alliance before the working alliance is firmly established, interpretations that point out a person's inconsistencies ought to be carefully avoided until the working alliance is solid.

The lateness behavior in this case was more than a reflection of a fear of dependency, as confirmed in later sessions; this lateness also reflected a growing feeling of anger towards the therapist. In the person's history the therapist mentally noted that the person first had developed positive feelings towards her husband and then these feelings quickly had turned to anger after they were married. He wondered if the anger was reflecting the compulsion to repeat some pattern of relating and hence whether the developing anger towards him was a form of transference. In the ninth session the person was late. At the tenth session, when the person was late again, the therapist asked her if there could be any possible meaning to her lateness. When she hesitatingly said she didn't think so he suggested that the lateness could reflect her fear of becoming too dependent on him. This, she accepted without resistance, but then went on to complain about something her husband had done since the previous session.

At the eleventh session the person was on time, but was more overtly angry at her husband, describing how he "neglected" her. The person had such a "head of steam" that she spent the first two thirds of the session talking about her anger towards her husband. Eventually she paused, then started to report a brief affair she had been involved in a few years before. She said she fell in love with a man who was a friend of her husband, but after a short time her positive feelings also turned to hate. Sensing the emergence of data that pointed to repetition compulsion, the therapist made a linking response. He said, "You seem to be suggesting a similarity between what happened in your marriage and what happened in the affair, only with the affair the process went much more quickly." The person did not overtly accept the suggestion at the time, but revealed her acceptance of it by mentioning a broken engagement where the same pattern manifested itself. As the session ended the therapist was aware of three links which had been tentatively forged towards understanding the repetition compulsion of this person.

There was one further link the therapist could have made. He could have suggested that the relationship with him seemed also to be developing in a similar way to the relationship with her husband and her boy friends. However, even though the therapist was aware of the anger being expressed towards him in her lateness, it was, perhaps, wise he did not attempt suggesting this link because the lateness was probably insufficient evidence for her to accept such an interpretation. In later sessions evidence for negative feelings towards the therapist would emerge more clearly so he would have a better opportunity to forge yet another link in the repetition compulsion. Ultimately, for repetition compulsion to emerge fully it needs to arise in three major areas: "out there" (present or immediate-past relationships), "in here" (therapy), and "back there" (relationships with parents or parental surrogates). It does not matter in what order or how these elements emerge, although most resistance tends to come from "back there" or genetic linkage. The easiest links for a person to accept seem to be those related to "out-there" relationships that have similarities.

The therapist needs to be patient in forging the various links which eventually reveal the enormity and pervasiveness of the repetition compulsion in a person's life. Sometimes this takes years. The neophyte therapist tends to be premature in making linkage interpretations. It is one thing to be alert for linking material and slowly build a case for repetition compulsion as the links emerge, and another matter entirely if repetition compulsion is peddled as theory that the person is supposed to accept without sufficient evidence. The latter is an approach that invites abortions of the therapeutic relationship. Even where there is sufficient data, early attempts at interpreting repetition compulsion can threaten to undermine the working alliance and hence the therapeutic relationship. Generally, a solid working alliance is a prerequisite for the acceptance of repetition compulsion. Prior to therapy the person can avoid facing the true extent of effects of repetition compulsion by a variety of defenses such as denial and repression. Therapy in the early part of the middle phase tends to erode these defenses and hence tends to make the person feel worse and not better. It should be noted that the eroding of defenses is not done at the initiative of the therapist. As material unfolds in therapy sessions that uncovers repetition compulsion, defenses will be weakened, particularly denial and repression. This can leave the person feeling vulnerable as is reflected in the comment, "I'm not sure this knowledge is doing any good because I feel helpless to correct the situation." Persons can feel they are actually getting worse and not better. So it is important that the working alliance is solid and that the person trusts the therapist, before any complete uncovering of the hold of repetition compulsion on the person.

It is natural for the person to discover the negative aspects of repetition compulsion first. At the time realization of the power of repetition compulsion occurs, the therapist needs to point out that there is a positive element to it. The repetition of the original situation where something unsatisfactory occurred is itself a part of an attempt to master or rectify the situation. Hence, the person unconsciously seeks other persons with qualities to enable the original traumatic drama to be reenacted. The unconscious hope, of course, is that in the new situation the ending will be different from the original ending. One 32-year-old woman with a passive-dependent personality sought therapy because of a frustrating relationship with an extremely compulsive, once-divorced man a few years older than herself. It soon became clear that he sadistically "put her down" whenever he had the chance, although it took her almost a half a year to verbalize this to the therapist because of her fear that the therapist would also "put her down." Another link in the repetition compulsion came when it was discovered she had been through an abortion after her lover abandoned her, once he learned of the pregnancy. It took more time before she became aware of how much her mother had "put her down" all of her life, and how strong was the desire that her mother change. After this genetic link was made the therapist raised the question as to whether the mother, who was over 70, could reasonably be expected to change. It took many more sessions before a major step in breaking the power of the repetition compulsion was taken when the woman gave up her need to see the mother changed. As a child the desire to change her mother was a reasonable wish; as an adult the change was no longer necessary.

The need persons have to compulsively repeat some traumatic relationship leads to some distorting of significant life relationships, especially in marriage and employment situations. Such distortions, which can be expected wherever there is a compulsion to repeat, are often referred to as transferences. However, they are not really manifestations of transference, but of transference-like behavior. Technically speaking, transference is a term reserved for the distortions that occur when a person is in a therapeutic relationship. Pastors, whether pastoral specialists or not, need to know about transference-like behavior because such behavior can often distort the relationship they have with their parishioners. In fact, pastors, more than other professionals except perhaps doctors, are the most susceptible to the distortions that occur in transference-like behavior, all pastors need to understand more the vicissitudes of transference that occur in the therapeutic relationship between pastoral therapists (and other therapists) and persons who seek their help.

Otto Fenichel (1945) gives the classic definition of transference. He says, "In the transference the patient misunderstands the present in terms of the past; and then instead of remembering the past, he strives, without recognizing the nature of his action, to relive the past and to live it more satisfactorily than he did in his childhood. He transfers the past attitude to the present." Chessick (1974) focuses on the resistance role of transferences "in which the patient defends himself against remembering and discovering his infantile conflicts and reliving them." Greenson (1968) indicates that the singular noun transference is actually misleading. Transferences, the plural, take place in the therapeutic relationship which consist of feelings that are inappropriately intense, ambivalent, capricious, or tenacious.

Two major ways of distinguishing transference is to speak of positive or negative types. Positive transference is where the patient feels love, fondness, trust, amorousness, liking, concern, devotion, admiration, infatuation, passion, hunger, yearning, tenderness, or respect. In negative transference the client has feelings of hatred, anger, hostility, mistrust, abhorrence, aversion, loathing, resentment, bitterness, envy, dislike, contempt, or annoyance. In intensive, uncovering pastoral therapy both forms of transference will appear, but it should be noted that the traditional image of the pastor as the ideal good parent makes it difficult for a person to express negative transferences in the presence of the pastor. Also, pastors themselves traditionally find being an object of hate a particularly difficult experience because they are often drawn into the ministry with a desire to be like a good and loving parent who cares for people.

Transferences that occur in therapy are often of a transitory nature so that many different kinds evolve during the course of a working alliance. However, a transference neurosis is another matter. In the transference neurosis the transference with the therapist takes precedence over everything else in the person's life and is a lot more difficult for the therapist to handle. The transference neurosis is more the phenomenon of classical four- or five-times-a-week psychoanalysis, but it can occur in intensive, uncovering pastoral therapy where the person is seen twice a week, and it will sometimes occur even when the therapist sees the person once a week or less. Therefore, the pastoral therapist needs to be aware of it so that it can be interpreted to the client as it commences to develop. If, when the interpretation is made, the client's (ego) defenses seem unable to stand the strain of the transference before it gets resolved, efforts may need to be made to break up the transference by decreasing the frequency of the treatment, by giving support, or by simply shoring up the person's defenses. Pastors who do not attempt intensive, uncovering psychotherapy or even brief therapy are not necessarily immune from experiencing transference-like neurosis from parishioners. One pastor, in his late 40s, who had developed some skills as a sensitivity-group leader, was invited by a pastor in another state to help him share in the leadership of a group marathon in his church where the group met from Friday evening through Monday evening of a long weekend. The group experience seemed to satisfy most of the members, but one of the married women in her late 30s with four children, verbalized a lot of positive feelings towards the sensitivity-group leader during the course of the marathon. The extent of this transference, which had rapidly blossomed into a transference-like neurosis, was not understood until a month later when the pastor–sensitivity-group leader noticed the woman in his congregation. At the conclusion of the service the pastor talked with her for a few moments and discovered to his consternation that the woman had purchased a home in the area and had persuaded her whole family to uproot because of her need to be near the pastor. This example is, unfortunately, not rare. Unless a pastor avoids dealing with people altogether she or he runs the risks of such transference-like neuroses. When such a transference-like neurosis occurs there ought to be an attempt to openly explain the possibility of what is occurring and if necessary, with both spouses present. What also needs to be understood is that this experience is not necessarily bad. The positive side is that the transference reveals the need the person has for psychotherapy and a possible readiness by the person to undertake it. Such a situation, skillfully handled, can lead to an effective referral. (Referrals are discussed at length in chapter 8.) What too often is seen by pastors as a disaster is really a golden opportunity to get someone to the help she or he needs.

Another way the transference will manifest itself is by the client demanding some kind of gratification during the therapy session such as being held in a lap, being hugged, having a cigarette lit, being helped on with a coat, having sexual intercourse, or receiving promises of marriage. This demand for gratification by the client must be distinguished from a certain amount of natural gratification which is built into the therapeutic relationship itself. There is gratification for the person in being able to have the undivided attention of the therapist for 45 minutes once or twice a week, in having material brought into the sessions looked at from the perspective of what is in her or his best interests, and in being able to express herself or himself unfettered by social restrictions.

One reason why demanded gratification is different from natural gratification is that denial of demanded gratification will generate in the person considerable rage. A pastor is often uncomfortable about having such rage expressed at her or him, so will often agree to a demand. However, from the point of view of therapeutic progress, direct gratification on demand is considered detrimental to the resolution of the underlying and nuclear conflict. This is because it reduces the immediate awareness of the depth of the conflict and hence reduces motivation for change of the underlying character patterns. To be able to resist the gratification demands of a person in therapy means the pastoral therapist needs considerable (ego) strength, as does the person underoing therapy. Of course, if the transference demands are too great, the therapist may be forced to shift to a more supporting role, at least for a while, but even in the more supporting, noninterpretative role, it is desirable to avoid gratifying such demands as much as possible.

When transference is getting too intense, one of the most effective ways of relieving it is by an attempt at a "genetic reconstruction." In a genetic reconstruction the person is encouraged to focus on other possible situations in the past where a similar feeling occurred, especially where the incident involved one or both of the person's parents. Whether the person can actually recover a past incident or not, the maneuver is often successful in relieving the transference feelings because the pastoral therapist reveals she or he is trying to understand rather than trying to seduce or be angry with the person, as the person has incorrectly perceived is the case. However, while the aim of such a maneuver is relieving of some of the intenseness of the transference, it should not be forgotten that the chief asset of the pastoral therapist is her or his ability to be a transference figure, to tolerate it, and slowly allow the transference to be resolved by the person herself or himself as she or he develops more effective ways of coping with situations.

Sometimes it is difficult for the person seeking help to see that transference is taking place, especially where projection is heavily used as a defense. For example, a man and his girl friend had planned a task together, but this had to be canceled when the girl friend became ill. The anger of this man, which had been heavily denied in the past, was far out of proportion to the frustration involved. As he himself indicated, it was unreasonable for him to blame his girl friend because she was genuinely ill and had not malevolently planned the illness. Unreasonably, he felt anger towards her and blamed her for his anger. When the person was able to acknowledge his own unreasonableness, the therapist indicated that it was this quality of the anger that pointed to transference feelings that were being projected into the present conflict. The therapist pointed out how important this incident was because it was not easy to find such a clear and convincing example of transference. The person accepted this interpretation, became a little excited, and then went on to describe, in contrast, an incredibly muddy situation where it was easy to blame the policeman who gave him a traffic ticket for speeding or his girl friend for sending him on the errand that resulted in the traffic ticket. But, as this incident was discussed, the man realized that the "arrogant look" of the policeman was a projection of his anger and that his girl friend had nothing to do with his traffic violation. His anger was all out of proportion to the event and, hence, was also transference. This then led him to explore his feelings towards the therapist and towards his mother.

Another case of unadulterated transference was clearly revealed when the person turned up at the wrong time for a session. The therapist, in opening the door of his office was confronted with two clients, one for whom the hour was her regular time, the other for whom this was a shift in time from the regular session, which he had noted in his date book at the request of his therapist, as he thought. This second person or the therapist had made a mistake about the shift of time. At the next session the therapist asked the person how he had felt about the mix-up and received the reply, "It's O.K., mistakes happen." But the therapist, sensing that the person had been angry, was not satisfied with this reply. He asked the person how he had perceived the therapist's response to the mix-up. The answer was immediate: "You were very angry. It was on your face." The therapist, who had not been angry when the two clients were in his waiting room, was able to state that this was not so and suggested that this person's perception was pure projection. Suddenly the person realized that the therapist was not lying, had no reason to lie, and that he, the person, had, in fact, been projecting his own anger which was basically a repetition of how he handled anger in growing up. With a wife or employer it was not clear whether the anger was projected or not, but in therapy the fact of projection could not be denied. In accepting this fact the person was able to weaken the transference.

Another example of the unearthing of transference comes from Irwin Singer (1970). A therapist had moved his office from one suburban location to another. He had mimeographed detailed instructions for reaching the new location and had given them to all patients before moving. A woman patient who seemed dominated by an unconscious and unadmitted conviction that she must never depend on anyone, came to her first appointment at the new office over half an hour late. She arrived feeling angry. She insisted that her "worst fears" about the therapist's inadequacy had been justified because he did not even know how one could reach his office and had given wrong directions.

"You should really know the difference between left and right! You must make a *right* turn at X Street to get here and you printed here make a *left* turn!" she exclaimed, pushing the printed instruction sheet at the therapist. He looked at it and returned it, asking her to reread it. After considerable effort the patient realized that she had misread the directions; they actually did call for a right and not a left turn. This little incident proved a turning point in her therapy, for it finally became apparent to her that she was terribly eager to distort in order to prove the inadequacy of any man—the therapist, her husband, a friend, or a colleague.

In addition to transference, countertransference is another way distortions occur in the working alliance. As Chessick (1974) indicates, "in broader terms, countertransference is thought of as a manifestation of the therapist's reluctance to know or learn something about himself." Singer (1970) says that "countertransference is similarly a device employed by the therapist to avoid his anxiety, to avoid threats to his own self-esteem and approval." One of the clearest definitions of countertransference comes from Jurgen Ruesch (1961). He indicates that "countertransference is transference in reverse. The therapist's unresolved conflicts force him to invest the patient with certain properties which bear upon his own past experiences and so his reactions are not wholly reactions to the patient's actual behavior."

A key question that the possibility of countertransference raises for the pastoral therapist is not, "Can I help you?" but "Can I stand you?" For pastors who seek training as pastoral therapists, the shift from the notion of "help" is rather difficult to make because helping is deeply embedded in the pastor's role through which the psychodynamic needs of those "selected" for ministry are culturally reinforced. When help is the focus of the relationship, the therapist can only permit a positive transference. This means that the person cannot use all of the therapist, but only the "helpful" part of her or him, and, in turn, this encourages the splitting of the transference and the need to have someone else persecute the person, generally the spouse. Hence, where the only transference the therapist can tolerate is a positive one, the relationship with the spouse or boss can deteriorate as the "therapy" progresses. Frankly, it makes a lot of sense for pastors not to dabble in intensive uncovering psychotherapy unless they are prepared to undergo years of their own intensive uncovering psychotherapy and then have years of competent supervision.

Menninger (1958) has compiled a useful list of the most common ways countertransference manifests itself in therapy.

1. Inability to understand certain kinds of material that touch on the therapist's personal problems.

2. Depressed or uneasy feelings during or after sessions with certain patients.
3. Carelessness in regard to arrangements—forgetting the patient's appointment, being late for it, letting the patient's hour run overtime for no special reason.
4. Persistent drowsiness of the therapist during the session.
5. Over or under assiduousness in financial arrangements of the patient.
6. Repeatedly experiencing neurotic or affectionate feelings towards the patient.
7. Permitting or encouraging acting out or acting in behavior.
8. Trying to impress the patient or colleagues with the importance of the patient.
9. Cultivating the patient's dependency, praise, or affection.
10. Sadistic or unnecessary sharpness towards the patient in speech or behavior or the reverse.
11. Feeling the patient must get well for the sake of the therapist's reputation and prestige.
12. Being too afraid of losing the patient.
13. Arguing with the patient, or becoming too disturbed by the patient's reproaches or arguments.
14. Finding oneself unable to gauge the point of the optimum anxiety level for smooth operation of the therapeutic process.
15. Trying to help the patient in matters outside the session such as in making financial arrangements for housing.
16. A compulsive tendency to "hammer away" at certain points.
17. Recurrent impulses to ask favors of a patient.
18. Sudden increase of decrease of interest in a certain case.
19. Dreaming about the patient.
20. Preoccupation with a patient or his problems during leisure time.

Chessick (1974) has developed a useful way for the pastoral therapist to monitor her or his countertransference and check the possibility of the therapist acting-in. He says the countertransference will be reduced or prevented from being destructive if the therapist a) is never exploitative or retaliative towards the person, b) acts towards the person like a guest in her or his home with her or his spouse present, and c) does not behave with the client in such a way that she or he would be unwilling to have it generally known to her or his colleagues.

One of the most common blunders of a pastor who attempts therapy under the rubric of counseling, is the sharing of her or his own problems. This is countertransference. If it occurs during a pastoral encounter or pastoral care of a few sessions, generally no harm comes from such countertransference, and occasionally something constructive may result. However, in attempting personality change, especially without professional supervision, such countertransference can create havoc in the life of both the client and the pastoral therapist, or at least block any chance of change in the client. This is because the countertransference is often the result of overidentification with the person and is, therefore, an attempt at getting too close to the parishioner. This is a defensive maneuver on the part of the therapist to deal with some underlying anxiety that is being stirred by the person's anger. By getting close the therapist is able to make it more difficult for the person to express her or his anger at the therapist.

The more intensive (two or three sessions a week), or the longer the therapy, the more countertransference needs to be monitored. This fact is highlighted by a Roche report (1968) which stated that the closer the examination and questioning of cases that continued over five years, the more unusual the needs of the therapist and the knottier the transference and countertransference difficulties. In one therapist who had a case for eight years, it was discovered that the therapist had omnipotent strivings to get patients "weller than well." He was "unduly over-protective, perpetuating in himself and in his patients an unspoken belief that his continuing ministrations through weekly visits, which had become more a ritual than psychotherapy, would magically ward off the return of the dreaded psychosis and/or hospitalizations." This same therapist was always accommodating by suggesting that the patients call him, telling them he could call back. He encouraged and perpetuated the excessive dependency.

From what has just been said it could be construed that the countertransference of a pastoral therapist must be avoided at all costs. This was the position of the early psychoanalysts. However, later psychotherapists have come to recognize that countertransference can be neutralized as the distorting force in the therapeutic relationship if it is recognized. One of the main roles of an experienced supervisor is to help the pastoral therapist get in touch with her or his countertransferences. However, the position taken in this chapter follows that of Edward Tauber and Maurice Green (1959) which goes one step further. The unearthing of counter-transference is not just to neutralize it, but where possible, to turn it into a useful constructive force in therapy. For example, a 25-year-old female therapist worked with a 19-year-old female schizophrenic patient who had a need to sit in the therapist's lap. The therapist permitted this regression to occur as it seemed to help the patient and led to less destructive acting-out behavior during the time on the ward she was not in therapy. After some time the patient started to fondle the therapist's breasts. In supervision the therapist indicated she was willing to allow this behavior because she felt comfortable with it. After several more sessions when the patient caressed the therapist's breasts, the therapist felt herself becoming sexually aroused, and, because she felt uncomfortable about this arousal, decided to tell the client about these two feelings immediately, without requesting any ceasing of the client's breast touching. The client, however, did stop the fondling and sat in silence for a few moment. Then she said, "I guess I may not be so bad after all." When the therapist got her to elaborate she explained that she had always felt her own sexual feelings were bad, but that if the therapist was able to have sexual feelings and lead a healthy life, there was hope for her yet. This is what is meant by not just neutralizing the situation. If neutralizing had been the goal, the therapist, upon feeling the arousal, would have set limits by asking the patient to stop and left it at that. Of course, the same insight may have emerged if the patient asked why the therapist had set limits, but most patients do not have the (ego) strength to ask that question. Hence, the therapist's sharing of her feelings allowed the patient to use the countertransference constructively.

Using the word "comfort" in the preceding illustration was no accident. One of the simplest and most effective ways of monitoring countertrans-ference is for the pastoral therapist to get in touch with how comfortable she or he feels. The concept of comfort is also much easier to use in communicating to persons than the term countertransference. For example, in a TV special Sammy Davis, Jr. stopped the show and suggested a change to the orchestra. He apparently was not feeling comfortable about something, because he said to the millions of TV viewers, "If I don't have fun, you won't."

Alfred Flarsheim (1972) makes a big point of the therapist's comfort level. He said, if the therapist is comfortable, both physically and emotionally, the countertransference problems are generally minimal. Flarsheim reinforces his point by describing the work of ethologist George Schaller who spent time living in close contact with gorillas in their natural habitat. Schaller's position was that in order to observe gorillas at close range, he had to go into the jungle unarmed. If he had carried a weapon, his own psychological state would have provoked retreat or attack by the powerful animals. But, unarmed, he had to depend upon his ability to adapt to the gorillas, respecting their behavioral communications so that he could retreat without provoking them.

Schaller's work is extremely suggestive for those who would be sensitive to the needs of mentally ill or distressed persons. *When one has no power over another person and no gimmicks, one is forced to observe more carefully.* It is such an observational frame of reference that makes the difference between whether the person moves toward wholeness or not. Using this concept, countertransference would be defined as anything that moves the therapist out of the observational frame of reference. Another way to state this is that as long as the therapist is learning something from the person the therapy will be basically constructive.

The following is an example of pastoral countertransference. The "therapist" was a male, single student-pastor in his mid 20s who was still attending seminary. Without any supervision, he consented to see a single, adolescent female. During the fifth session, she suddenly burst out crying. When he asked her what was wrong, she told him that she had been to the doctor the day before and discovered she was pregnant and was now fearful of being found out by her parents or other people in the church. When he asked if she knew the father of the pregnancy, she was uncertain. She wanted an abortion and was prepared to pay for it with savings. The primary difficulty was the state where she resided would not permit the abortion (at that time, liberal abortion laws had been enacted in some of the other states). The "therapist" agreed to help the young woman by suggesting he take her to Mexico to have the abortion.

There are many features of this attempt at therapy which could be discussed. Assuming the best course of action was the abortion (this was inadequately explored), there were many other ways for the pastor to help the client to Mexico without taking her himself. This move on his part indicated countertransference which came from his overidentification with her as a person wishing to avoid dealing with authorities like her parents, just as he had avoided supervision by an authority. There were many things that needed to be explored with this young woman by a competent therapist, but these needs were neglected because of the young pastor's unawareness of his countertransference.

If developing a working alliance, maintaining structure, and helping a person find the way in which a repetition compulsion occurs in her or his life are major tasks of the first half of the middle phase of therapy, interpreting distortions that occur as a result of the compulsion to repeat and helping the person develop new adaptive patterns are the major work of the second half. This says a lot in one sentence. Interpreting the distortions that occur because of transference needs skill and timing that generally only experience can bring. In practice, making the person aware of her or his distortions means interpreting the person's defensive maneuvers. Before this can be done effectively, the pastoral therapist needs to get in touch with any distortions that are arising in the relationship because of countertransference. If this has been done, then a distortion that occurs in the session must be a distortion that the person is making as she or he views the nature of the relationship with the therapist. The pastoral therapist can more clearly discern a person's defenses when she or he has dealt with her or his own countertransferences.

Interpreting defenses needs further explicating because the neophyte pastoral therapist can all too easily turn the process into a confrontation battle. The interpreting of defenses is generally done after the pastoral therapist has patiently waited for a situation to develop where the data will be clear and obvious when pointed out to the person. The person will often give little clues so that the pastoral therapist is aware of the rationalizations, projections, denials, reaction formations, or whatever, long before a clear example emerges. Data which are convincing to the therapist whose professional task is to look for defenses are often not sufficiently clear to the person in pastoral therapy. Further, trying an interpretation, and "trying" is the word, requires a sensitivity to the readiness of the person to accept the interpretation. The way the person tends to handle such interpretations has already emerged in having to deal with any initial resistance to being evaluated or to the working alliance. If such initial resistance and the defenses involved have been overcome, the defenses that have emerged in conjunction with the transferences of the middle phase can also be changed. The initial resistance, however, is only looked at sufficiently to enable the evaluation to occur, or for the working alliance to develop. In the latter part of the middle phase defenses and distortions involved are raised and interpreted repeatedly as the person attempts to form new adaptive patterns of behavior. At this stage the therapy has more of a conditioning flavor to it.

Lest conditioning be seen as negative, rat-like, inhuman, impersonal, manipulative, and controling, one should be reminded that what is done within a therapeutic relationship of trust with the cooperation of the person as a willing partner, is an entirely different matter than the fantasies associated with the robots of a mindless society. Much of the second half of the middle phase of pastoral therapy is the unique form of conditioning for which pastoral therapists ought to make no apologies, and which was long used before the more systematic investigations associated with behavior modification took place.

Another form of distortion is transference-like behavior. The pastor, by virtue of his position or her position as a leader of a congregation, gets transference-like responses from both the church and the community. These are inappropriate or irrational feelings that parishioners or community members express towards the pastor either verbally or in writing. The following letter is an example of positive transference-like behavior where the dynamics are fairly obvious.

Dr. Jones
First Methodist Church
Young Town, U.S.A.

February 4, 1976

Dear Dr. Jones:
Many people may come to you for guidance, for help in moments of sorrow, for enrichment of their lives to become a member of a divine church and faith.

I'm turning to you for the desire to express my appreciation— my appreciation for the fine organization and inspirational presentation of the Sunday morning worship service. The bulletins are written in a form easy to follow. The prayers of confession are beautifully composed. The choice of songs always familiar and loved. Your sermons are always interesting and something I always wish to remember. All prayers, all directions, all songs presented by the choir, and scripture lessons and sermons are delivered clearly and meaningfully. I think you and your staff do an excellent job.

I regret my neglect of going to your services before now. I normally only attend church when I go to my former home, where my Methodist membership is present. I wish to thank you for my spiritual awareness being deepened in the four services I have attended this year at your presiding church.

With deep sincerity,
Judy Smith (Mrs. A. R. Smith)

P.S. I have a pleasure I would like to share with you. This coming Saturday my husband is returning home after spending 13 months overseas with the U.S. Air Force. I am beside myself with happiness that this past year is behind us and we can return to sharing our lives.

What this letter indicates is the need everyone has at times to externalize the source of feelings in someone or something concrete and then express them towards this "object" as a way of dealing with those feelings. If Mrs. Smith's husband had been killed on duty, she probably would have needed an external source for blame, to whom she could express negative transference-like feelings. As the author wrote this very point, he was on board an airplane taxiing along a runway before taking off for Chicago. The plane suddenly stopped and the hostess came forward to ask that the passenger destined to Pittsburgh push the call button. Everyone laughed, but no one moved. Confused, the hostess went to the Captain's cabin and returned to announce, "Sorry, computer error!" The computer in modern society is becoming an acceptable source for a lot of transference-like behavior, especially the negative form (scapegoating). Whatever the theological reason for the existence of a devil or demons, the psychological need for such externalization is obvious if the distortions involved in transference and transference-like behavior are understood and taken seriously.

The idea that the pastor is a recipient of much positive and negative transference-like behavior is not new. Efraim Rosenzweig (1941) expressed the view that people see the pastor as a father-authority figure who is representative of God. On the one hand he gets veneration and respect, on the other, resentment and hostility. This ambivalence, according to him, is often acted out in church divisions where some are fanatically loyal to the pastor and others are so negative they form splinter groups. Since Rosenzweig wrote about this many churches have developed multiple-staff ministeries. In churches with pastors, and especially when one is an older man and the other a young person just out of seminary, the stage is set for both the positive and negative sides of ambivalent transference-like behavior being externalized by parishioners, with one pastor being the "bad guy" and the other wearing a metaphorical white hat. Where this happens among individual parishioners, where the pastors understand the transference-like behaviors that are involved, and where they accept their roles as a part of their professional functioning, thus maintaining a healthy, open relationship with each other, no harm occurs. Moreover, with skillful handling many parishioners who need to use their pastors as "good objects," can be referred for the therapeutic help they need to make their internal psychological processes more integrated, and their lives more pleasurable and productive.

E. Mansell Patterson (1965) also discusses the role of the minister as an object to attract transference-like behavior. He thinks that the concept of parent-pastor conjures images that are parts of an undifferentiated identification system in the minds of many. Even when the pastor behaves in an innocuous fashion, she or he can be treated as if she or he were a monster. Sexual transferences often occur in which a woman who overvalues and overidealizes her father may almost worship a male pastor and see his wife as her (oedipal) rival. In extreme grief situations a parishioner may curse both God and pastor alike, accusing the pastor of all kinds of neglect. Elderly persons often see their young pastor as the good or faithful son who will not desert them, and then get upset when he moves to another parish. As more women are ordained and function in parish settings, many more mother-associated transference-like behaviors are anticipated to emerge in both men and women parishioners.

Patterson helpfully lists a number of signs of transference-like behavior for which pastors can be alert.

1. Frequent visits by a parishioner for individual attention.
2. Where the pastor is present in a parish group and a person reacts differently from the rest of the group.
3. Overly protective or negative responses to routine pastoral work.
4. Requests for counseling in unusual places, times or situations.

5. Demands that the pastor resolve personal problems or make personal decisions for the parishioner.
6. Failure to keep appointments or fulfill obligations.
7. Overscrupulous performance of duties, especially if related to pastor's work.

Little has been said about the pastor's countertransference-like behavior in the literature, so a few examples are listed here.

1. The pastor becomes obsessed about one of his parishioners so she or he is continually on his or her mind.
2. Looking upon a person or persons as being the saviour of the local church she or he serves.
3. Getting sexually involved with her or his parishioners.
4. Finding herself or himself getting unreasonably or irrationally angry with a parishioner.
5. Using a parishioner as a special confidante.
6. Needing praise from her or his people all the time.
7. Constantly watching to see that a coalition is not forming to ask her or him to leave.
8. Being reluctant to visit the hospital or go near certain kinds of people.
9. Overly conscientious in enforcing denominational needs on the local congregation.

Donald Williamson (1967) sought some experimental verification of the transference-like objects and hypothesized that the minister and someone else, his wife or a leading layman, were cast by parishioners in positive and negative transference-like roles. He then tested out this hypothesis using 60 members of the leadership structure of a large, Midwestern Methodist church.

In his experiment he used what is known as the Buss aggression machine which supposedly gives a small electric shock of an intensity varied by the person administering the shock. Each of the 60 persons in the study was told that she or he was involved in a teaching experiment where she or he was to shock the person (pastor, lay leader, or lay person) on the other side of the machine when that person made a mistake. The pastor, lay leader, and lay person were all instructed to make the same mistakes. Of course, the shock connections had been secretly disconnected. When the intensity of the shocks were observed, it was found that the pastor's mean shock level was significantly lower than either the lay leader or the lay person. This was seen as support to the idea that he was the "good" transference-like symbol in this church. The lay leader, on the other hand, received a mean shock score significantly higher than the pastor or the lay person. He was the "bad guy" in the church situation and the receiver of considerable negative transference-like behavior.

What follows is an example of a negative transference-like behavior experienced by a pastor in training, in his own words.

> I was asked to return and conduct a seminar during the fall retreat of the youth group of the church. In fact, the church offered me the job of minister of youth because the previous pastor wanted to become the full-time Christian education minister.
>
> One week before the seminar I was asked to attend a meeting with the youth minister and the mother of a girl who had signed up for a weekend retreat. We met in the youth minister's office. The mother was defensive because the pastor was reluctant to have the girl attend the retreat. She said that her daughter simply clashed with the youth minister because of his dogmatic personality. This sounded reasonable because I also thought he was too dogmatic. Then the mother said that her poor baby girl never had a father because the "bum" was a professional golfer who traveled nine months every year, and he would only drink or beat the mother or daughter when he was home. So, they were divorced five years ago. After two hours of tearful talk we decided to let the girl go on the weekend if she would agree to participate and not argue.
>
> The retreat was great. The girl tried very hard to be positive. I spent a few hours each day talking to her, trying to build a relationship for the time when I would be asked to become the youth minister. She responded positively.
>
> The first three months of my ministry with the group was also positive. She didn't attend anything regularly but she would drop in sometimes and share her opinion about things. Then one night she came to my Bible-study group and afterwards I selected a group of teens to help me with a project. She was not on the list. She became angry and in front of everyone started screaming that I didn't love her, that I only selected my 'favorites.'
>
> Two weeks later she came to another youth meeting and

while I was preaching she started screaming at me that I was a hypocrite, that I hated her and she didn't give a damn. She ran out of the church saying that she would never come back again. I was embarrassed and torn apart wondering what I had done to the girl to cause such a reaction.

A few weeks later her Sunday-school teacher arranged a special dinner for this girl and myself at the teacher's home. It was a wasted supper. The girl eventually began swearing at me and screaming that I hated her. She kept saying, 'You say you love me but you don't show it. You're just like all the rest of those damn men.'

After this experience I talked to Dr. Smith [the pastor's supervisor] because I couldn't control my reactions to this girl. I was nervous, threatened, and constantly thinking about the girl and where I did wrong. Dr. Smith explained that everything pointed to transference-like behavior. The girl was transferring her bad childhood feelings about her father onto men in authority positions, such as the previous youth minister and myself.

Since then, I have had a few encounters with this girl but I must confess that now her screaming is over, I do not have to 'own' all of the garbage she dumped on me, and that is a relief.

These words speak for themselves. When this pastor understood that transference-like feelings were involved, he was freed from his countertransference-like feelings of responsibility and guilt and hence, from his immobility.

In another example, a pastor needed the liberation that can come from realizing that transference-like behavior is at work. The pastor belonged to a religious faith group noted for its strict teetotalism, yet which also took seriously the Sacrament of Holy Communion which was given with unfermented grape juice. However, as an acting out of feelings towards his parents, this pastor one Sunday served real wine at a Communion service. The pastor did not consciously anticipate the angry response of his congregation which eventually led to his removal. His bewildered response indicated that he had acted more unconsciously than anything else and pointed to the need of psychotherapy to resolve the problem underlying the countertransference-like behavior.

Hopefully, enough has been said about transference-like and countertransference-like behavior to confirm what most pastors have experienced in their ministry. It supports the contention that a pastor who denies or avoids dealing with transference-like behavior in her or his parish can be made to feel miserable. It is the stance of this chapter that both the parish pastor facing transference-like behavior and the pastoral therapist confronted with transference, are dealing with a similar problem. However, it is the author's contention that the parish pastor's problem will often be more difficult to handle than the pastoral therapist's problem because the therapist, through establishing a firm frame or structure, is able to interpret the transference for the distortion that it really is. On the other hand, if the nontherapist attempts to interpret transference-like behavior as transference, it is often not clear to the parishioners involved that this is so. Many young pastors with little or no training in pastoral therapy make the mistake of using interpretation in their pastoral role without the structure of a therapeutic relationship and a working alliance. Interpretation under these circumstances is generally not only ineffective, but often "backfires" because the parishioner's transference anger, reinforced and legitimized by the anger generated by the pastor's "meddling," gets acted out in the church community. Such persons try to generate allies to form an "anti-the-pastor" group. Not all splits that occur in churches come from badly handled transference-like behavior, yet transference-like and countertransference-like behaviors play a major role in many of the splits that occur in churches and demand a lot more attention from parish pastors than they now get. While pastoral therapy does not offer a model for handling transference-like behavior that can be copied by pastors involved in pastoral care, an understanding of this phenomenon should also lead to an understanding of why interpretation outside of therapy will generally not be effective in handling transference-like behavior of the parish. However, pastors not acting as therapists have other ways of handling such behavior. For example, if the social nature of the parish makes acting-out more difficult for the pastor to deal with, it also provides the pastor with a powerful means of dealing with persons. Working through small ad hoc task forces and committees is perhaps the best way to deal with transference-like behavior that has become entwined in local-church politics.

Another process that distorts the therapeutic relationship and has application for parish pastors is externalization. Anna Freud (1965) coined the term when she discovered children who used the therapist to represent some split-off and unacceptable part of their own personality. In a sense externalization is linked with projection. Instead of distorting the reality of a situation by projecting a feeling or thought onto someone as a defense against something inside herself or himself, the person selects someone who does have the undesirable qualities. This enables the person to avoid looking at the same qualities in herself or himself. In this way externalization theoretically could be conceived as a nondistorting relationship because the externalization does not involve a distorting of the person's perception of herself or himself. However, when the other person in the externalized relationship does not match the needs of the person completely or changes over a period of time, projection generally takes place to bridge the gap. Hence, where there is externalization, projection is normally involved also, and hence, more obvious distortion creeps into the relationship.

Projection is only one technique to maintain externalization of some unacceptable part of a person. As Warren Brody (1965) indicates, some people are adept at continuing to manipulate reality so that the externalizing defense can be maintained. To the extent that other persons can be kept functioning in a certain role, the person does not have to use projection in the sense of imputing behaviors or attitudes that do not exist. One of the principal ways to manipulate others into externalizing roles is through control of information. It is no accident when couples come to a marriage counselor with marriage problems that one of the biggest complaints is lack of communication. There are a lot of other reasons for this, but many wives and husbands have the need to keep their spouse in the externalized role.

The concept of externalization gives one another way of looking at the distortion of transference in pastoral therapy. Where the positive transference comes as a result of the externalization of the good elements of the person's character, it is possible for the relationship with the therapist to make the person feel worse because all that the person can experience once the therapy gets under way is the bad aspects of her or his own personality. Many pastors, who, without training or supervision, have seen their parishioners for several sessions in a pastoral-care basis get false courage to continue the sessions on a regular basis because of some immediate relief the person feels from the "honeymoon effects" before the transference involving externalization develops. However, as the sessions continue, the pastor finds to her or his consternation that the care and attention that is given no longer seems to help. The nicer, more caring, and more concerned the pastor becomes, the worse the parishioner feels because of the splitting that is occurring and because of the externalization processes involved.

Perhaps more importantly externalization is a reason why many parishioners who need therapeutic help never get it. A study at the Menninger Foundation (Kernberg et al 1972) indicates that one of the best prognostic indicators for psychotherapy is the capacity of a person to think psychologically, that is, to see the locus of the problem as inside rather than being "out there." As will be discussed in chapter 8, one of the greatest tasks in making a referral for psychotherapy is to help the person see that the problem is inside herself or himself. Externalization is a special problem for pastors, marriage counselors, and medical practitioners because persons coming to them generally blame an external event or another person for their problems and therefore come seeking an external form of dealing with the problem. Either the person seeks the manipulation of the external situation or asks for a prayer or a pill to do the change for her or him. Until this externalizaing concept of both diagnosis and treatment is understood as resistance to personal change, such persons induce therapeutic misalliances (Langs 1976) as a resistance to the working alliance. When work and the notion of partnership or alliance is stressed, the person is really being asked to give up the notion of an external force or magic that will actually do the changing for her or him. For the religious person the issue is not whether God is going to change her or him or heal her or him, but how God is going to effect the change.

Some persons, in asking for help, don't really want to be changed; they want the restoration of the status quo. Where this is an appropriate goal, the pastoral encounter or a few limited sessions of pastoral care, and reinforcing the externalizing mode, may be the most effective way of helping the person reach this goal. However, where the goal of the intervention is to change the person's personality structure in some way, either through brief therapy or through intensive uncovering, pastoral therapy, the person will need the capacity to shift away from externalizing defenses towards introspection.

Before the conclusion of this chapter on distortions, it needs to be said that positive and negative transference reactions normally occur with persons of a neurotic personality structure. One new line of thought from the Chicago psychoanalyst Heinz Kohut (1971) is that the narcissistic personality has a transference relationship with the therapist that is not along the classical lines. He suggests that the two kinds of transference that occur in therapy with a narcissistic personality are what he calls mirroring transference and idealizing transference.

The mirroring transference is generally what the narcissistic person seeks first. The therapist focuses on the accomplishments of the person and gives her or him the praise and "stroking" for which she or he hungers. The person does not present each week in the therapy session with her or his problems, but with the successes. The person needs someone to acknowledge how great she or he really is. Lest the reader should misunderstand, it needs to be said that the therapist is not asked to say anything false or insincere. It is just that in life the ordinary person holds back from so much stroking in order to prevent giving the other person "a swollen head." Mistakenly it is thought that praise and recognition create the narcissism; whereas it is hunger for the recognition that creates the narcissist's way of talking about herself or himself. The healthy person, listening to the narcissist, soon tires of giving an inordinate amount of stroking, and where this happens, the narcissist experiences more rejection, more wounding, and a greater hunger for recognition as a way of compensation. In the transference with the narcissistic personality, then, the therapist is to so mirror the interaction that he gives the person the recognition for which she or he hungers. One example of this was the young person, who, when he started to get the mirroring from the therapist, appeared the next session with his guitar and played to his special audience of one the whole session. Then there was another client who presented his manuscript of poems to get the recognition for which he craved.

What needs to be seen is that the narcissist risks rejection and wounding when she or he allows the mirroring transference to develop. Expecting rejection as a way of repeating the past, she or he may even try to manipulate rejection if feeling the therapist is gaining too much power. If the maneuver to reenact the repetition-compulsion through rejection is interpreted and hence thwarted, then two things will happen. First, the relationship will move from a mirroring one towards an idealizing transference. The person thinks that if the therapist is able to recognize and accept the person's greatness, then the therapist herself or himself must be great. The second thing that follows is an attempt to make sure the therapist as an ideal source of gratification is not lost or does not "die." Therefore, the person tends to incorporate within herself or himself this idealized figure as a way of insuring that the figure is preserved, and from that point the therapy moves more along classical lines.

The narcissistic personality is mentioned in this chapter because it illustrates a special way the therapeutic relationship is distorted, and gives an example of a transference that will be increasingly discussed in therapeutic textbooks. It is also mentioned because pastors regularly encounter narcissistic-like transferences in parishes, and because a pastor herself or himself can often seek a narcissistic relationship with her or his own congregation as a way of getting the gratification for which she or he deeply hungers. Where narcissistic-like transferences occur, the pastor would do well to recognize them, and when they are severe enough to force her or him to choose between persons, referrals need to be made. Also where the pastor is too dependent on the affection and admiration of her or his parishioners, a therapeutic relationship is generally needed to resolve her or his own narcissistic relationship with the congregation and generate a healthier form of ministry.

7 : Termination

After the middle phase pastoral therapy moves naturally into the termination phase. When does this take place? Chessick (1974) says, "Psychotherapy is really a never ending process." The question of termination is not "when is your psychotherapy over?" But, "when is it no longer necessary for us to have formal meetings in order that your psychotherapy process may go on in a continuous fashion?" If one accepts Chessick's understanding, one is still left with the question of when the formal therapy sessions are no longer necessary.

Frieda Fromm-Reichmann (1950) suggests that the formal sessions can end when, a) the person has sufficient insight into her or his own relationships and dynamics to handle life situations adequately, b) when the person has achieved the goal of the contract, and c) when the person has resolved transferences and distortions.

Another way of stating the "when" of termination is to cast it as a question of freedom. The person is ready for termination when she or he has independence from previous hateful or loving attachments to her or his elders and gains a nondefiant sense of self-value, free and apart from their judgment; and when the person no longer needs the approval or disapproval of authority figures and does not fear retaliation if something is done without their approval. This enables the person to be able to freely give and secure love and to develop durable relationships of intimacy.

Carl Whitaker, the University of Wisconsin family therapist, has a perceptive way of determining the point where the need for termination arises. He identifies the beginning of the termination phase when he finds himself wanting to pay the client for the hour. This occurs because at the end of the middle phase the person is pulling earlier insights into a more comprehensive view of the whole process of her or his life and these insights contain a lot of material of theoretical importance to the therapist which can be used in teaching and publishing.

The goal of termination, as Chessick (1974) points out, is not the termination of psychotherapy, but the termination of sessions with the therapist. Terminations that are most likely to be successful are those where the decision to terminate occurs naturally and jointly. If the therapist decides the termination arbitrarily, the person is, in effect, infantilized and forced to choose between passive compliance or defiant rebellion, or to just regress in such a way as to bring on a recurrence of all the old symptoms. If the person suddenly decides to terminate it is generally as a defensive maneuver to avoid painful material. This is discussed under premature or abrupt terminations.

The author's preference is to talk about the necessity of termination when the goals established during the initial phase are met. This may mean that the therapy is terminated without complete resolution of a transference as indicated by Fromm-Reichmann (1950), and may indicate incomplete autonomy of the person from parents or parental figures, but be appropriate to the goals of the brief pastoral therapy. Therefore, in describing the necessity of termination when the goals of therapy as established in initial phase are reached, one is able to have an understanding of termination which covers brief pastoral therapy, supportive pastoral therapy, and intensive, uncovering pastoral therapy. As a lot of pastoral therapy is of the brief kind, the definition of termination being related to reaching the goal set in the initial phase of therapy is a preferred way of viewing termination.

One variation to the idea that therapy terminates when the goals of the contract are reached is the possibility of recontracting. This may occur during the course of middle phase in brief pastoral therapy if the person becomes aware that there were other tacit goals behind the request for pastoral therapy which only emerged as the middle phase continued. Thus, pastoral therapy that commences as brief therapy with a specific goal in mind can evolve into intensive, uncovering therapy provided this is made clear as the need is revealed and both parties are able to accept the new contract. On the other hand, pastoral therapy that has commenced as intensive, uncovering treatment can and does get recontracted into brief pastoral therapy with specific goals where it is obvious from the therapeutic interaction that the intensive, uncovering pastoral therapy has a poorer prognosis than when first evaluated. Under these circumstances the recontracting occurs naturally during the course of the middle phase.

For example, an energetic secretary, married and in her mid 40s, sought psychotherapy for the purpose of helping decide whether she wanted to go ahead with a divorce or not. She had filed for divorce 12 months previously but had become overcome with doubts and uncertainty about her action. The brief psychotherapy contract was to help her discover what she really wanted and then help her achieve it. After 40 sessions she had sorted out all of her options and had expressed many of her feelings, particularly the anger she felt about being controlled by an infantilized relationship with her husband and by an unreasonable and demanding father. However, before the divorce was obtained, the woman came to realize that she wanted more than just help with the divorce. One weekend, she was visited by her parents who, while she was shopping, altered the sleeping arrangements in the apartment. This incident brought out a torrent of anger in the therapy session against the interference of her parents and their way of infantilizing her. It was then she became aware of the need to resolve her long-standing dependency on her parental figures and contracted for pastoral therapy focused on characterological change.

It needs to be emphasized that when the specific, goal-oriented, brief pastoral therapy successfully reaches its goal and then a new goal suddenly emerges, the suddenness suggests that the new task be explored as resistance to the terminating of the relationship.

After the goals of therapy have been reached, further sessions should be continued until the relationship between the person and the therapist is resolved. If the pastoral therapy has been brief, say 20 sessions, one session generally will be enough to dissolve the real attachments of the therapy relationship. However, where the pastoral therapy has been intensive, uncovering, and consisted of two or three sessions a week for three or more years, three months at least should be taken in the termination phase of the pastoral therapy. This is because the cessation of long-term therapy is a replica of a death experience of a love object, especially a parent. The three months of termination sessions gives the person time to anticipate the grief process. It also gives the person time to deal with the impending loss through the introjection of the therapist. This is like saying that while the external object of the therapist will die when the interviews end, the person is able to memorialize the death, not by a slab of marble, but by the parts of the therapist that live on in the mind and heart of the client. The introjection of the therapist is intended to be a healthy, normal, and useful way of terminating one of the most meaningful relationships the person may ever have. By allowing for the internalizing of the therapist, reinforcement is given to the fact that the psychotherapy can continue as an internal process without the need for even occasional sessions. Most persons who have been through successful psychotherapy can testify to the experience of talking to their therapist in their own mind when they get caught in a crisis or in a situation that has similarities to a pattern involved in the repetition compulsion.

The Bible is familiar with this process of introjection. For example, in the shephard's psalm the words are: "Yea, though I walk through the valley of the shadow of death, I will see no evil, *for Thou art with me*." This suggests that in the funeral service where these words are spoken, grieving persons are given support and encouragement in the introjecting process. But for the therapist one of the best ways to help a person in the termination phase with the introjecting process is to help her or him resolve any negative feelings about the impending loss.

Long before the termination stage is reached, however, the person can be prepared. A skilled pastoral therapist will take the opportunity afforded by any interruptions to the treatment through her or his absence either by illness or by vacation to have the person express any anger felt for having disruptions to the therapeutic process. An alert therapist will treat these as mini-termination experiences and as a foreshadowing of eventual termination. Thus, through having the person ventilate anger over sustaining the loss of an important relationship, the person is able to retain her or his feelings of affection, respect, and admiration of the therapist, free from her or his negative attitudes.

One of the prerequisites for a successful termination is sufficient notice of the actual termination date. After a mutually agreed upon decision that termination will be taking place either at a specific date or around a specific period of time, the termination process is similar whether it takes three months or more, or is compressed into one session. As Freud indicated, beginning and ending therapy is like chess where in the opening and closing phases there are a limited number of semiritualized moves. For the sake of clarity what happens in the final session of brief pastoral therapy will be described in some detail.

At the beginning of the last session the fact that this is the last session needs to be verbalized. It is the therapist's task to communicate this to the person if the person is reluctant to acknowledge this as fact. The therapist does this by reminding the person that the date has been reached that was mutually agreed upon earlier for the termination of the therapy. In this way potential resistance to the termination will generally be surfaced at the beginning of the session and thus dealt with during the session while there is time.

The next step is to handle any anxieties that may surface openly or indirectly. If anxieties about the termination of therapy are mentioned openly, they can be discussed with the attitude that separation anxiety is normal and natural. If these anxieties are expressed indirectly as the presentation of new material, the new material can be handled through "slotting." By slotting it is meant that the person is stopped after a few moments and it is stated that this material belongs in a certain general area (slot). If possible, the person is reminded that the problem is similar to another discussed earlier under that particular topic, and this is usually enough to stop the flood of new material. If the anxiety is expressed as dependency and gets focused as some kind of uncertainty about coping, some form of *realistic* assurance is in order, like, "Based on the insights and behavior of the last months (or years), you have the tools to cope a lot better than before." Yet another way the anxiety of termination may appear is in the return of symptoms. These are dealt with by indicating that this sometimes happens and that soon after the last session the symptoms should start to diminish again.

By far the most important task of the termination session is to encourage the person to review the process of therapy. As this reviewing process develops, the therapist could add more material and turn the session into an interaction between two equals who are rehearsing a meaningful experience together. This review is similar to the reminiscing of the aged in their preparation for death. It assists in the process of introjection that is taking place. It reinforces and stores the highlights of the relationship into deeper recesses of the brain. Sometimes the session has about it a feeling of celebration, especially if the therapy goals have been completely reached.

As the session draws to a close, it is appropriate for the therapist to express any genuine feelings of appreciation and to receive any the person may want to give. All that then remains is for the therapist to give the final word of assurance that she or he is always available should there ever be a need to return. The following is the write-up of a termination of brief pastoral therapy.

Write-up No. 10

Identifying Information

    Session: No. 13 (termination)

    Date: June 12, 1976

    Place: First Methodist Church, Milleageville, Georgia

    Client: Mrs. Patrick

            644 Clay Street, Milleageville, Georgia

            Phone: Home—DE 6-4340

    Work:—DE 6-4000

    Pastor: George Tweedledee

Initial Behavior

    Mrs. Patrick came 15 minutes early. When she came into the room she quickly sat in the soft chair and started talking immediately.

Initial Words: "*I'm afraid I have lots of problems this week!*"

Declaration of Purpose: The pastor reminded Mrs. Patrick that the session before they had together decided that this session was going to be the last one.

Dealing with Termination Anxiety: When Mrs. Patrick agreed, the pastor then wondered what the meaning of all of these new problems were. She did not know exactly what he meant, so he asked if she was feeling anxious about the termination. She didn't know for sure, she said, but then went on to say that she had been wondering all week if she was going to be able to cope with things once the relationship was terminated. The pastor then assured Mrs. Patrick that he had been impressed with the change she had made and felt that she had a far better chance of coping this time than she had before.

Review of the Therapy: In reviewing the course of the therapy Mrs. Patrick indicated that the most important discovery was that her husband really did care for their daughter and therefore did care for her. She also felt that the selling of the camper had shown that her husband could be flexible and additionally had relieved their financial problems. She realized now that she had more power over her husband than she had given herself credit before. She went on to say that she had asked for a $40.00-a-month allowance from her husband, and that while he had refused, she only considered this "round 1" instead of surrendering to him like she used to do.

Towards the end of the session Mrs. Patrick talked about her bachelor uncle's recent behavior at a funeral where he was rude and rather exhibitionistic. When she patted him on the knee to try and shush him he had been embarrassed by her intimacy. She said she realized that he wanted attention but not closeness. The therapist asked if she was indirectly communicating something else. This led her to get in touch with the fact that she felt her husband rejected her need for closeness, but that this was not a desire to reject her personally because of anything she did, but because of his own development in childhood. She seemed to accept the lack of intimacy on his part as being less personally aimed at her than she did previously.

Leave-Taking: At the end of the session the therapist shared how he had enjoyed working with her. She thanked him for the therapy which she had experienced as being worthwhile. The therapist indicated that she seemed to be now in touch with inner feelings and hence had resources for coping in the home and at work. If she ever needed the resources of the church, they were available to her.

In brief pastoral therapy of 13 sessions, taking one session to terminate is generally all that is necessary. However, as a general rule, the longer the pastoral therapy, the greater the number of sessions necessary to terminate. Persons seen even in brief therapy sometimes need more sessions to terminate. Essentially the same dynamic process takes place as in one termination session, but the extra sessions are necessary for the termination to feel comfortable to a particular person and to work on termination dreams. In longer therapy, especially intensive, uncovering psychotherapy, not only does the termination take longer, but sometimes a "tapering off" process is purposely proposed by the therapist or even suggested by the person. The sessions can be first reduced from twice a week to once a week. Sometimes, the therapist may eventually schedule a session three months or even 12 months ahead. If the person is ready for termination, the therapist will no longer be needed as a transference figure. However, during termination the therapist can reinforce this by being as natural and human as possible, sharing perhaps more of herself or himself than would be appropriate in the initial or middle phases of the therapy. Following the suggestion of John Hinkle, a faculty colleague, the author encourages the client to send a card at Christmastime. Some pastoral therapists eventually become a social acquaintance of former clients, especially in a church setting where the pastoral therapist is on the staff, but it needs to be remembered that where this happens it may be difficult, if not impossible for the therapist to be used as a therapeutic resource in the future. Pastoral therapists need to explain this to the person during termination when the suggestion of a continuing social relationship occurs. It is then up to the person to choose whether she or he wants to risk losing the therapist as a therapeutic resource. Naturally, sometimes the therapist is not interested in continuing the relationship on a social basis, but if the therapy has been successful, this fact will not be an embarrassment to anyone.

Premature termination attempts are common in psychotherapy. Essentially premature termination is the attempt at terminating a relationship before the goals of the contract are met. The premature suggestion can come from either the therapist or the person. When it comes from the therapist the person may acquiesce, but not really be ready for termination. Careful attention to the person's dreams and behavior (for acting-out) can reveal the person's true response to the suggestion of termination. If the therapist has greatly misjudged the situation it would be profitable for her or him to explore further her or his countertransference feelings. When the suggestion of premature termination comes from the person, this needs to be seen as resistance to remembering something important which is handled through acting-out and leaving therapy. Exploration to find the reason for the premature termination attempt can often be very productive of significant material which otherwise would probably not surface. Sometimes the premature termination occurs because the person feels the therapist does not have the skills necessary to take her or him through pastoral therapy to a completion. With a well-trained, experienced pastoral therapist, this situation probably would not arise. However, it is just another form of resistance or transference. Fortunately, in many cases, where relatively untrained or unsupervised pastors are in "over their heads," the person as the (ego) strength to terminate prematurely. In the sense that the goals of therapy were not reached, such a termination is premature, but from the point of view of reality some of these premature terminations are long overdue.

Abrupt terminations are a special kind of premature termination. They vary anywhere from the person who suddenly fails to attend the therapy sessions, or who phones to say she or he is not coming to sessions anymore, to the person who unexpectedly announces at the beginning of a session that this will be the last session. Abrupt terminations are a sign that the therapist has missed some essential ingredient to the therapy. Because of the abruptness of the termination, which is generally an acting out of feelings rather than a verbalizing of them, it is difficult for the therapist to handle, especially if she or he is already blind to some important dynamic that has led to the termination of in the first place. Under these circumstances often the best the therapist can do is to try to get one hour with such a person in an attempt to find out the meaning of the abrupt termination. This is the obvious course of action where the person comes to a session and suddenly announces that it will be the last session. If after spending approximately half the session exploring the meaning of the person's behavior, the person fails to reveal what it is, or is still determined to terminate even if the reason is not given, then the therapist needs to go through an abbreviated termination routine after accepting any negative feelings that the person may have. Even when the person may feel that the negative aspects of the therapy outweigh the positive elements, the course of the therapy can still be reviewed as a part of the terminating process. As one former supervisor once explained to the author, even if the case has been thoroughly bungled, there is no excuse for not terminating the whole process correctly.

It is not the major goal in an abrupt termination to persuade the person to stay in therapy; it is, however, important to seek the meaning behind this acting-out behavior. Where the meaning of the behavior is explored, the person will sometimes gain considerable insight and may or may not elect to remain in therapy. Whatever happens, it is important for the therapist not to defeat this insight process by having as a secret task the retaining of the person in therapy "come what may." When the person fails to say she or he not returning it is the task of the pastoral therapist to try to get the person to return for one last terminating session. Even if the person is noncooperative in finding the meaning of the abrupt termination, it is often helpful for the person to feel she or he has fulfilled an obligation made during the contracting part of the initial phase by returning for a final session, and thus is able to terminate the therapy without any feeling of guilt. Where the person has suddenly dropped out of pastoral therapy without a word, it is the author's practice to make one phone call or drop a card indicating that the request for termination indicated by the behavior is acceptable, but that she or he should return for the last session in order to wrap things up as promised as in the original contracting. A large percentage of persons abruptly terminating with no warning or communication will respond to such a request to honor the contract when the request is done without the intention of manipulating the person to stay in therapy.

Abrupt terminations need a psychotherapy postmortem. In one case a 26-year-old single male with a depressive neurosis in an obsessive-compulsive personality trait disorder, who underwent intensive, uncovering pastoral therapy for 12 sessions, abruptly terminated therapy with one session's notice. When the supervisor asked the therapist about the case, she discovered that the therapist had heavily interpreted the person's intellectualizing defenses and had insisted that the person get more in touch with his feelings. When the supervisor asked why the therapist had been so aggressive in the case, the therapist could only answer that he was impatient with waiting out the obsessive-compulsive personality and that he had wanted to explore the possibility of some shortcuts in therapy with such persons.

The issue of this case centers around the therapist's strategy of working for congruence between thoughts and feelings. Technically, the therapist may have been right in having as one goal the congruence between the intellectual thoughts and the feelings of the obsessive-compulsive person if this is her or his frame of reference. However, the strategy of the therapist in the first part of the middle phase raises the question of whether the therapist had developed a working alliance and had helped the person uncover the compulsion to repeat. The therapist said he thought he had a good working alliance with the person but later admitted he had not reached first base with the compulsion to repeat. He also had received no dream material in this case. As the supervisory session developed the therapist became aware of his angry countertransference feelings towards the person and how he had been subtley seduced into replaying the original role of the parent figure in pressuring the infant to produce, in this case the infant's feelings. The repetition compulsion was occurring in the therapeutic relationship and hence was blocking the establishment of a good working alliance. Under these circumstances it is not surprising that there was an abrupt termination when the therapist went on to deal with the matter of congruence before adequately dealing with the matter of the working alliance and the compulsion to repeat.

The therapist took one step further in understanding what had taken place in this case when he realized that he, himself was going through a state of transition including remarriage and how this had affected the case. Much of his impatience came from his own feelings of insecurity. Hence, his own personal situation made him more susceptible to the problems of countertransference. The therapist was experienced enough to know that there is very little that can be done to hurry a person with an obsessive-compulsive trait disorder and therefore some countertransference feelings must have been operating.

In another abrupt-termination case, a 39-year-old woman with two children terminated after four sessions. She simply did not appear for the fifth session. When the therapist and supervisor did a postmortem on the abrupt termination, it was noticed that in the third and fourth sessions the woman had taken a lot more trouble to dress herself attractively. In the third session her voice was huskier and she had openly talked about divorcing her husband. It was then conjectured that she had terminated to avoid a strong sexual transference neurosis with the therapist. When a follow-up contact was made accidently, all she would say was that she terminated the sessions because they made her "too upset." The therapist accepted this explanation so as not to reinforce any feelings of guilt and shame.

Forced terminations (Langs 1974) present problems for pastoral therapists. Such terminations occur through external circumstances such as an unavoidable move by the person to another area for business reasons, or termination from therapy because of a changed financial situation. Forced terminations also occur because the pastoral therapist completes a practicum at a counseling center or finishes a degree and moves to a new position. When such forced circumstances occur the person generally experiences a lot of murderous rage which gets expressed in a variety of ways. It will generally help the person if the therapist can encourage the verbalization of the rage. It also helps for the person to receive as much notice as possible from the therapist is the forced termination comes about because of circumstances in the life of the therapist. It is also preferable if the person receiving therapy knows of any time limitation imposed by external circumstances during the initial phase of therapy and having the possible termination difficulties discussed as a structural arrangement then.

Having discussed the matter of termination, it is appropriate to look at the fifth kind of clinical writing, the closing summary, which should not be more than one page. The purpose of the closing summary is to have in the person's folder the material necessary to write a letter if this is called for well after the case is terminated. It is doubly important for a clinic to have such a summary in case the therapist leaves. It involves a tremendous amount of labor for another staff member to go back and spend hours reading the files before a letter can be written. In contrast, at the time of termination, the case summary would take a therapist familiar with the person about 20 minutes, and can generally be done with ease. The closing summary is also a way to help the therapist deal with the sense of termination.

A good case summary will tend to be no more than four paragraphs. There is no correct way to do this, but practice suggests the following order in which matters are covered briefly, yet comprehensively.

First paragraph: It includes the name of the client, the number of interviews, the dates of the first and last interviews, the frequency of the sessions, and source of the referral.

Second paragraph: It includes the presenting problem, a brief diagnosis, and the nature of the contract.

Third paragraph: It gives a summary of the therapeutic process, including an example of something that reveals what the client was like.

Fourth paragraph: It shows how the therapy terminated and any recommendations such as further therapy or referral.

As an example of a closing summary, the summary of the case of abrupt termination just discussed will be given.

Write-up No. 11

Closing Summary: Dec. 16, 1975 Mrs. Jones, a member of the Methodist Church, Central, Illinois, came for four interviews between November 24 and December 25, 1975. She was self-referred.

The presenting symptom was depression which seemed to have been connected to a marriage conflict which had openly existed for five years. Mrs. Jones gave evidence of having a depressive neurosis in a hysterical personality trait disorder. The contract was to explore the kind of help Mrs. Jones needed, pastoral care; supportive therapy; conjoint marriage therapy; brief, or intensive, uncovering pastoral therapy.

In the second session the depression started to lift and Mrs. Jones expressed considerable anger towards her husband. By the third session she started to develop a strong positive sexual transference neurosis with the therapist.

Mrs. Jones abruptly terminated after four sessions by failing to keep her appointment. In a follow-up contact Mrs. Jones indicated that the therapy was making her "too upset." The therapist saw the abrupt termination as a defensive maneuver to keep repressed her underlying conflicts. Brief or intensive, uncovering pastoral therapy is recommended if she ever seeks further help.

When everything else had been said about termination, it still is important for the neophyte therapist to realize that termination itself can be as productive if not more so, than any phase in pastoral therapy.

8 : Referral*

J udging from the professional literature, making a referral is a relatively uncomplicated matter. The helping professional simply suggests to the person seeking help that the help he sought from another recommended professional. Lest we overstate the case for the textbooks, it should be said that they imply rather than give this definition. The few texts in the therapeutic disciplines which mention referral at all, give the subject a cursory discussion. Lewis Wolberg's two-volume, 1500 page classic on *The Technique of Psychotherapy* (1954), for example, devotes two pages to the topic. It seems to take for granted that a professional competent enough to conduct psychotherapy will not find referral a problem area.

When we delve into the pastoral literature, we find that details on referrals are given more attention than in other therapeutic circles. Howard Clinebell (1966) and Thomas Klink (1962) have written two articles which contribute to understanding the referral process. Yet considering the way referral gets stressed in the training of ministers, the material on the subject is still meager and inadequate. This is especially regretable when we cannot assume that all pastors are highly trained psychotherapists.

Since the Gurin, Veroff and Feld study (1960) established the oft-quoted figure that 42 percent of people interviewed said they sought a minister as their first source of help, it has been assumed that clergymen are in a position to make more referrals than any other professional. Actually, only 9 percent of this

*Given as an address to the Pastoral Care Section of the Third Great Lakes Health Congress, Chicago, 1973 and published as "Referral as an act of pastoral care" in the *Journal of Pastoral Care*, Vol. XXX, No. 3, Sept. 1976. Republished here with the permission of the *Journal of Pastoral Care*.

number ever get referred to another professional. While ministers take evident pride in the fact that so many people come to them initially, other professionals have wondered what has happened to the other 91 percent. By far the largest group out of the 42-66 percent are generally non-referrable and have sought out the minister to request help in maintaining their present life-style. They have no thought of changing their basic personality structure and a referral in their case would constitute an inappropriate response to their call for help. I will focus briefly on this group, but I wish to spend the greater part of the paper on the referrals that the pastor has an opportunity to make, some of which are made successfully—the 9 percent in the Gurin study, and some of which fail to be made—25 percent that might be referred if ministers would improve their techniques and recognize their own resistances.

There are indications from the Gurin study that people seeking help from a clergyman generally seek ways to maintain themselves as they are, whereas those going to a psychiatrist are more open to changing their personality structure. It is significant that only 7 percent of those going to a clergyman said they sought to change themselves, whereas 22 percent of the people going to psychiatrists said they wanted to change. However, 80 percent of those going to a clergyman sought some kind of help for maintaining themselves, while the figure for psychiatrists is only 40 percent. Hence, referral by a clergyman often implies a major shift in the kind of help being sought. Many are not ready to make that shift and are not referred for this reason. There is evidence from the Gurin study to support the contention that many persons are satisfied with the maintenance style of help which they expect and receive from clergymen. Sixty-five percent of those who saw a minister said they were helped. They would see a referral to a psychiatrist, psychologist or social worker as unnecessary and inappropriate. Therefore, in the majority of these cases, the minister accepts the maintenance stance of his parishioners, knows they are not interested in depth work, and does not send them on to another therapist.

However, pastors do refer many people, and with good reason. The most obvious situation is that of a pastor confronted with someone whose problem goes beyond his professional training and competence. Yet there are many cases of referral which take place for reasons other than competence. Some pastors with excellent training deliberately limit the number of sessions and then refer as a way of sharing their skills with a maximum number of persons. Others with the training and competence deliberately limit the number of persons they see on a regular basis. Further, because of a parishioner's friendship or position in the church, the pastor may wish to refer. Or it may be that, while the pastor is technically qualified, he may not feel there is sufficient mutual liking for the establishment of a therapeutic alliance with a specific person, and hence decide to refer.

Sometimes a pastor resists referring a parishioner when there is a need to do so. Resistance to referring someone traditionally comes under the topic of countertransference. Simply stated, countertransference consists of the needs and feelings evoked in the pastor which impede what needs to be done in the best interests of the person or client. Competent supervision, collegial or interprofessional consultation, and/or psychotherapy are some of the best ways of helping to resolve the pastor's countertransference problems. Specifically, the countertransference will be felt as fear in one form or another. The pastor fears the shame which he feels as a consequence of his "failure to help." He fears the guilt which comes from feeling that he has caused the parishioner's difficulty by inappropriate pastoral help which will get exposed in a referral. Sometimes he fears the loss of his relationship with his parishioner. Or he fears that the psychiatric relationship will be a destructive one, especially because he does not know the psychiatrist personally.

One reason why a pastor may not make a referral when he needs to do so is because he doesn't realize the seriousness of the situation. He lacks diagnostic ability and hence is not able to recognize the severity of the symptoms. Yet while pastors may not be formally trained in differential diagnosis, they should be able to recognize their own feelings of being scared or seduced or manipulated. In other words, it does not necessarily take training in diagnosis and dynamics to recognize the need for referral. Those who are resistant to knowing themselves and their own feelings are the ones most likely to resist referring their parishioners.

The reverse side to knowing oneself is the feeling of omnipotence. Persons with omnipotence needs are often attracted to the ministry where the role of being a totem for the church community invites all kinds of projections, magical expectations, and transference-like behavior. The role in which parishioners tend to cast their pastors can feed and nourish these unresolved omnipotence fantasies. Such omnipotence is displayed in the need to be not only "all powerful," but "all saving" and "all healing" by the magic of word and personality. For pastors with these dynamics, making a referral is very difficult because it is tantamount to an admission of defeat, and it would be very threatening to admit such powerlessness because the feelings of omnipotence are often in themselves a defense against the helplessness of unresolved dependency needs.

It is one thing to seek to deal with one's own resistance to referring; it is another to deal with the resistance of the parishioner or client. I believe it is basically a problem of resistance—the clergyman's or the parishioner's—which keeps a good share of those 25 percent who might be referred from seeking further professional assistance. Slowly we have learned that making a referral is a lot more than just recommending another professional. It basically means dealing with the emotional resistances to the recommendation. There has been a myth that it was those pastors without special training who referred the most. However, we now know that it often takes a great deal of skill and all the professional training a man has to be able to accomplish a referral. Referral itself is skilled work and should be regarded as an act of pastoral care.

Although it does not take training in diagnosis for a pastor to know when he needs to refer, it does take training to be able to make effective referrals. Once we view referrals, not as something separate from treatment, but as a topic within the dynamic structure of a counseling-therapeutic relationship, one of the basic problems related to referral is dealt with. Like counseling, referral has an initial, a middle, and a termination phase. Like counseling, an evaluation is made in the initial phase. The evaluation may take a few minutes or it may be very thorough and take four or more sessions. Once the evaluation is made and it is decided a referral is necessary, the work of referring becomes the work of the middle phase. A skilled practitioner keeps the focus on the goal of referral and tries to deal methodically with the resistances to being referred. Pastors with a capacity to do this find that most of their referrals reach the source of help being recommended.

Often a person who comes for help will perceive or feel the referral as an act of rejection. He may see himself as someone bad or unacceptable or sick who has to be gotten rid of as soon as possible. (This is what going to a psychiatrist still symbolizes for many people.) And, it has to be admitted that some professionals, including pastors, unconsciously or consciously use referral as a means of getting someone "off their backs." They don't care where the person goes as long as he doesn't come back to them. But when the referral itself becomes a process which may take many sessions to deal with, the person seeking help has a chance to experience the referral as an act of pastoral caring, not rejection. The very fact that the pastor takes the time and trouble to deal with the resistance becomes an indication that he really does care and is referring because he honestly believes that the person to whom the referral is made is in a better position to help than he is.

The major reason for resistance to a referral on the part of parishioners is the expectation they bring to the initial interview. They expect that they will be helped by the pastor. This was documented in the data from the Gurin study which stressed that maintenance was a major goal in seeking help from a clergyman, whereas personality change was the main expectation in seeking help from a psychiatrist. Any attempt by a pastor to refer to a psychiatrist or psychologist may carry with it an implicit shift in the kind of help being sought. Unless the goals involved in seeking help get dealt with as a part of the referral process, many people may get lost in the shuffle and never reach the recommended psychiatrist. Sometimes we have to deal with the unrealistic and magical expectations that parishioners and others have of us as pastors before persons are ready to see they are going to need the kind of therapeutic experience for which a referral to a psychiatrist is necessary.

The distinction between personality maintenance and personality change affects more than the referral process. There is evidence from an 18-year study at the Menninger Foundation that these concepts are related to treatment outcome (Kernberg, 1972). As indicated earlier in the Gurin study, one of the ways we seek to maintain ourselves is to see the source of the problem in the external environment. However, change in personality involves being able to identify the internal factors

contributing to conflict, and this often constitutes a radical shift
from the focus with which the person originally seeks help. The
Menninger study concludes that patients who were able to
decrease the extent to which they externalized responsibility
were able to significatly improve their functioning in society.
Those who, at the beginning, were able to internalize, or were
able to make the shift toward internalization, had the best
chance of improvement.

We are suggesting here that working with a parishioner to
help deal with his resistances to referral involves more than just
making a referral. We begin working on the externalizing style
that many persons bring to the helping relationship. The task of
referral which is accepted as an act of pastoral care is more than
just seeing that a relationship with another professional takes
root; it begins the process itself through encouraging the client
to deal with conflicts in their internalized form. By focusing and
working on the feelings involved in resisting the referral, the
client is encouraged to look within.

Over the last 20 years the Pastoral Psychology Department at
Garrett Theological Seminary has made many referrals of
students to therapists in the local community. About half of
these referrals involve students who want therapy for training
purposes, the other half show a wide range of psychotherapy
(Christensen 1958, 1960, 1961, 1963). Out of our experience
with approximately 500 cases, we have been able to draw some
conclusions.

1. *The chance of a successful referral is enhanced if the
professional to whom the referral is made is personally known
to the one making the referral.* Nonverbally we communicate a
sense of confidence which is difficult if the referral is to an
unknown person. Furthermore, the development of relationships between the faculty of the Department and the professionals in the community has led to vital feedback. We have
developed some skills in knowing which students work best
with which therapists and this has led to more and more
successful referrals and has increased the effectiveness of the
therapeutic outcome. Furthermore, the professionals have
gained more confidence in the evaluative judgments of the
pastoral psychology faculty and hence respond with slightly less
reserve to a referral, which in turn contributes to referral and
treatment success.

2. *That the chance of a successful referral is enhanced when a positive transference is present.* Mr. Jones, a student of considerable ability, developed some unrealistic criticisms of his teachers. At the same time he overidealized one of the pastoral psychology faculty members. As the year went on Mr. Jones became more conflicted, depressed and work inhibited. He eventually sought out the faculty member whom he idealized and was referred to a community therapist, with good results.

3. *That the chance of a successful referral is enhanced when the client or parishioner is given an honest, straightforward evaluation which neither exaggerates nor minimizes the situation.* Such tactics as exaggeration or minimizing may manipulate a person to see a therapist, but they generally establish dynamics which eventually hinder treatment or lead to an abrupt termination. In giving an evaluation we would avoid technical terms yet try to make clear the seriousness of a problem and what options a person has. We have discovered that the kind of person that we picture as not accepting our recommendations for referral before we given them, is the very person who needs all the honesty he can get, but with kindness and in languages he can understand.

Admittedly, such an honest evaluation can evoke anxiety and anger, but these reactions become the focus of the referral process. We welcome them because they lead us to the referral resistances which have to be dealt with, and hence to the heart of the person's problem. Miss Williams was a lesbian whose behavior made the administration uncomfortable. Because the administration insisted she see the Counseling Department, her motivation for treatment was questionable. Nevertheless, an extensive evaluation was made which included some psychological testing and a history.

In the evaluation session Miss Williams was told that therapy was being recommended because of her impulsive, immature behavior which led to constant conflicts with friends and others with whom she tried to establish a relationship. Miss Williams burst into an angry tirade at the counselor giving the evaluation. She indicated that she did not need treatment but only an acceptance by society of her homosexual condition. The counselor indicated that the evaluation was responding to her feelings of extreme misery, her suicidal thoughts, and her jealous feelings which seemed to tear her apart. He said he was not primarily concerned with her homosexuality. Despite her abusive behavior, the counselor kept to his position, not as absolute truth but as an evaluation made to the best of his professional ability. Miss Williams terminated the interview by walking out, slamming the door, and screaming a few insults.

Miss Williams rejected the referral but remained a student. Eight months later she made an appointment to see the counselor and he prepared himself for another round of abuse. Miss Williams appeared on time and was calm and relaxed. She said she had made the decision to seek treatment and wanted the name of the person to whom she had been referred previously and had forgotten because of her rage at the time. She reported that every time she had been miserable, which was frequently, the words of the counselor's evaluation came to her, not as rejection, but for their honest acceptance of her real situation. She found strange assurance in the fact that someone had not flinched at taking her abuse but had tried to represent a touch of reality. She wanted him to know this and encouraged him to continue this kind of evaluation process. In the Department's experience, a small but important percentage of referrals are of this delayed variety.

4. *That the chances of a successful referral are enhanced by the use of the "relay" technique.* As you know from athletics, in a relay race sprinters run parallel until a baton is transferred. In a similar fashion the person referred may see both the referring and referred-to professionals concurrently for a brief period of time. The case of Mrs. Smith is reported in detail because it not only illustrates the usefulness of the relay technique, but also illustrates many other aspects of the referral process.

Initial Interview—January 1967

Mrs. Smith was a vivacious, well-groomed, fifty-year-old woman who came to Rev. Green, the minister of counseling in a large church, as a referral from the senior minister, who had seen her twice but was made anxious by her suspicious thoughts and her story that she had been in a state hospital for mental patients. Mrs. Smith opened the session by saying that she had so much to tell she didn't know where to begin. Rev. Green indicated he understood from the senior minister that there was a question of whether she needed psychiatric help. After quickly agreeing, Mrs. Smith said her troubles began in 1955 when she was divorced from her husband in another state. Soon after her return to her home state she discovered not only glaucoma in her right eye, but a need for an operation on the left eye, which took away her peripheral vision yet enabled her to preserve the central vision of that eye.

The next thing Mrs. Smith mentioned was the trouble she had had gaining employment. Eventually she learned to be a typist in medical records, using a dictaphone. What led her to seek help from the senior minister was the feeling that people in her office were saying terrible things about her. When Rev. Green asked for the reasons which led her to this, Mrs. Smith was silent and a little confused. Rev. Green asked if she had had these tendencies before. Not only did she admit this, but Mrs. Smith went on to talk about her hospitalization in a state hospital in 1950. When Rev. Green asked her if she knew what her diagnosis had been, Mrs. Smith hesitated, and, looking carefully at him, indicated that she was labeled as having "paranoid tendencies." Mrs. Smith then described her hospital experience as being very unpleasant. While she did not have electric shock treatment, she had felt depersonalized, especially since she was retained against her will.

Rev. Green asked her about the last few years. Mrs. Smith said that last summer she got all "upset" again when a tornado came down near her home. After the tornado she went to see a Methodist minister in another church, and he tried to get her to see a psychiatrist. Later, when she visited her family doctor, he had given her the same advice, and, in fact, the name and number of a psychiatrist. Rev. Green pointed out that she had just been through a similar process with her present senior minister. To this Mrs. Smith replied by stating she did not like psychiatrists. When asked why, she indicated she feared they would hospitalize her again. Rev. Green asked if she saw things and heard voices. When she said she had none of that, Rev. Green indicated that he was doubtful if she would need hospitalization, especially as the present trend was toward out-patient rather than in-patient treatment.

Mrs. Smith was silent. Eventually Rev. Green said, "You know, Mrs. Smith, with the kind of troubles you have, especially these suspicions, you are likely to scare the non-psychiatric professional half out of his wits." She grinned and admitted that the senior minister had gone two shades of gray when she told him her symptoms. When Rev. Green said that she seemed to be looking for someone to help her whom she didn't scare, she laughed with what seemed like relief.

Rev. Green said that he thought it important for her to know that he would be moved by his Bishop in four months time. Therefore, what she needed was to establish a relationship with a professional who was going to be in the community a long time and who would not be scared by her symptoms. The best person to see would be a psychiatrist.

When Mrs. Smith indicated that she feared the psychiatrist would hospitalize her, she went on to say that probably a few more sessions with Rev. Green would be enough. At this point, the minister said that, when she got over her present upset, she should take the time to spend several sessions getting to know a psychiatrist. If she was well when she went, there would be no need for him to hospitalize her and he would become a permanent resource in the community for the periods when she became insecure and paranoid.

As time was up, Rev. Green suggested that Mrs. Smith come back in a week to discuss the matter further.

Comment:

In a session with his clinical supervisor, Rev. Green indicated that he had seen four options emerge during the first session as possible ways of helping Mrs. Smith. These were:

1. See Mrs. Smith on a short-term, crisis basis. The treatment would consist of support until she found a new job, became settled into it, and her paranoid symptoms decreased.

2. See Mrs. Smith for long-term treatment.

3. See Mrs. Smith for intermittent management on a long-term basis.

4. Referral.

Rev. Green said that because he was being transferred by his Bishop in a few months he had ruled out two and three as being real options for his relationship with Mrs. Smith. Furthermore, in view of the trouble Mrs. Smith had been through in locating someone she could trust, Rev. Green did not see the point of using crisis intervention alone as really meeting Mrs. Smith's long-term need for security. Therefore, he decided to refer to a local psychiatrist. He had indicated the need for referral to Mrs. Smith in the first session so that she did not become too attached to him, have her hopes raised, and thus provide further resistance to a later referral attempt. At the same time, he scheduled a further session with the intention of working out the resistances to the referral, especially her fear of hospitalization by a psychiatrist.

Second to Fourth Interviews:

Mrs. Smith was on time for the second interview and immediately spoke with great rapidity about all the problems she had had in her past. She started to elaborate on a long but interesting history. Eventually Rev. Green asked why she was giving all this material when he had indicated at the last session that she needed to see a psychiatrist. She said that she didn't want to see a psychiatrist and was still hoping that he would continue to see her and that she would be helped by him. After Rev. Green indicated that he had not changed his mind, he invited Mrs. Smith to talk more about her fear of psychiatrists. Mrs. Smith became more openly critical and hostile, enumerating the many ways she had been badly treated in the past. At the end of the second session she was invited to return again the following week to continue the discussion.

During the third session Mrs. Smith's hostility was greater. She became angry at the fact that she had to tell her story repeatedly as she sought help from first one person and then another. She also indicated that the problem with her eyes came from syphilis which she contracted when younger. For this reason, she said, she could not have children.

The same pattern of hostility came out in the fourth session. Toward the end of the session Rev. Green indicated that he thought their work together had gone about as far as it could go. He indicated that he was not prepared to see her anymore unless she would see a psychiatrist. Mrs. Smith immediately started to talk rapidly about being rejected at work. When Rev. Green suggested that she was avoiding the issue, Mrs. Smith remained silent for a few moments. She then indicated that she still feared unjust treatment at the hands of a psychiatrist, but would be willing to try once more. Mrs. Smith asked for and was given the name of a local psychiatrist who had achieved excellent results with other members of the church. Rev. Green suggested that he and Mrs. Smith meet again at the usual time the following week, but that the session be reduced to 20 minutes. The purpose of the meeting was for Mrs. Smith to talk about the progress of her arrangements for a referral. Mrs. Smith agreed.

Comment:

It is clear from the material on these sessions that Mrs. Smith consistently sought to avoid a referral. One of her methods was to control the conversation. After Rev. Green allowed some of this verbal control, he was able to indicate to Mrs. Smith that her need to see a psychiatrist would not go away by avoiding talking about it. This led to the expression of a lot of anger toward Rev. Green in an indirect and externalized form. Gradually, however, she displayed more anger in the sessions and had this anger accepted. As Mrs. Smith became more in touch with her anger she became less paranoid, more able to share sensitive matters such as her syphilis, and became more willing to see a psychiatrist. Hence, when Rev. Green became firm during the fourth session about a referral by indicating he would refuse to see her further unless she saw a psychiatrist, the prior work on her resistances paid off.

Immediately after Rev. Green's insistence that she see a psychiatrist, Mrs. Smith indicated indirectly that she was experiencing the referral as an act of rejection. Rev. Green countered this by scheduling a further appointment, which had the effect of communicating that he was not referring her just to get rid of her, but because he really believed it was in her best interest to be referred.

Fifth Session to Termination

In the fifth session Mrs. Smith indicated she had made an appointment with the psychiatrist but it was not for another ten days because only then did he have an opening. A 20-minute session was arranged for the following week.

In the sixth session Mrs. Smith was again able to express her anxiety about seeing the psychiatrist. Rev. Green indicated that now was the time to establish a relationship with the psychiatrist because of the decreased paranoid symptoms since she had first been to see him. He indicated that he was sending a brief letter to the psychiatrist. Mrs. Smith readily agreed and signed a release of information sheet. Mrs. Smith spent some time telling about her other job possibilities. A 15-minute appointment was made for the next week to report on the visit to the psychiatrist.

In the seventh interview, which was short and the terminating one, Mrs. Smith expressed a great deal of relief and joy. She liked Dr. Brown and felt he was kind, interested and skillful. She thanked the counseling minister for the letter he had sent which had saved time and money. She expressed appreciation for his help during a critical period.

While Rev. Green stayed at the church, Mrs. Smith attended morning worship. From quick sentences as she left the church he discovered she saw Dr. Brown another three times before terminating with him and felt she could go back to Dr. Brown any time she needed to do so. She had managed to get another job and felt more settled. Her paranoid symptoms had abated.

Comment:
In the fifth to seventh sessions the relay technique was used. By the time Mrs. Smith actually saw the psychiatrist, only one overlapping session was needed. The fifth and sixth sessions served to function as support until the psychiatrist could find a time when he could see Mrs. Smith. In continuing to see Mrs. Smith until she got to the psychiatrist, and in writing a letter to the psychiatrist about Mrs. Smith, Rev. Green again demonstrated that his referral was not an act of rejection. Further, he placed himself in a position of continuing the relationship concurrently with the psychiatrist if Mrs. Smith needed time to establish a relationship with him. He was also in a position to refer to another psychiatrist if Mrs. Smith could not establish a relationship with the first one.

In reducing the length of the sessions from fifty to twenty and then fifteen minutes, Rev. Green reduced the risk of his double message being interpreted as ambivalence or weakness. He was saying that he did care, but, because he cared, he was referring. Structurally he communicated he cared by simply continuing to see Mrs. Smith. Yet reducing the length of the sessions said structurally not to rely upon him as the principal source of help and therefore to take the referral seriously.

By the sixth session Mrs. Smith's presenting symptom of paranoia had almost disappeared. Rev. Green's work had helped her through the crisis situation. But by insisting on a referral he was able to utilize her experience of his helpfulness and her growing trust of his professional judgment to help her gain a resource that would be useful in the years ahead. In doing this Rev. Green turned a short-term crisis situation into a long-term gain. Now Mrs. Smith has a permanent resource for future intermittent management when her life situation intensifies her feelings of insecurity and leads to paranoid symptoms.

Referral is one of the most versatile techniques at the disposal of a professional minister. However, it takes considerable skill and training to utilize it to its full potential. Theological curricula in the practical field have been built on the notion that, while all students need to know something about pastoral care, only a few specialists would learn about the counseling process in depth. This conception does not work because referral, as an example of pastoral care, is subject to the same dynamic processes as one encounters in brief psychotherapy (Lewin, 1970). Hence, any attempt by seminaries to teach pastoral care divorced from teaching brief psycholtherapy and the supervision of case work will do little, if anything, to increase the referral rate from ministers to other professionals. It also does little to enhance the effectiveness of other pastoral care work.

This article has drawn attention to referral as an example of pastoral care rather than as an act of rejection. Referral is a process in which the resistances are explored and dealt with. It is enhanced by good relationships with the community's professional resources; by using the natural transference relationship which often exists with a minister; by skillful evaluation; and by the "relay technique." Of all the professions, perhaps ministry is where referral has its greatest potential. It is up to the minister to master its techniques as part of his professional contribution to the healing-helping arts.

Conclusion

When the processes of pastoral therapy in the preceding chapters are taught to rabbis, ministers, priests, and theological students, the fear is raised that they will be seduced away from the ordained ministry into one of the secular healing professions. While this risk is undoubtedly present, it is greatly exaggerated. After 10 years of teaching a pastoral therapy course the results are that the course decreased rather than increased the risk. The less a mystery is made of pastoral therapy, and the more obvious the long painstaking hours of labor involved in being obligated to clients, the quicker pastoral therapy loses its seductive quality. Conducting psychotherapy is dirty, dangerous work, spent in the "sewers" of people's minds. It requires much patience. The psychological risks, and the wear and tear on the therapist are reflected in the high suicide rate among psychiatrists. Only a few seem naturally endowed for this work, and even then they need a long, expensive period of apprenticeship. Rather than be seduced into wanting to be psychotherapists, pastors respond to the exposure to pastoral therapy material by appreciating more the work of therapists, by interacting more with professionals in their own community, and by making more referrals. They also tend to develop greater confidence in their pastoral care work.

Some pastors, without proper training, unfortunately, try to build a local church around a healing ministry alone, get in over their heads, and create a horrible havoc in the lives of many persons. Parishioners involved in such a church sometimes become very disturbed and often end up in the office of secular therapists, helping create a poor impression of pastors. The author knows of the seminary careers of three such "healing" pastors, all from different seminaries. They had avoided all classes in pastoral care and counseling and avoided the quarter's full-time experience as a chaplain in a hospital setting under supervision of a qualified supervisor, known as clinical pastoral education. Further, inquiries among persons who were the peers of these students in seminary revealed that these "healing" pastors were already convinced before entering seminary that God had given them special healing powers. They felt they did not need supervision; one actually volunteered to be a supervisor. It has to be understood that these pastors were students in the late sixties and early seventies when seminary curricula were forced by student pressure to have many electives. This made it possible for students with such grandiose notions to graduate from seminaries unchallenged. Those pastors who, without theory, supervision or personal therapy, are prepared to "experiment" beyond the bounds of traditional pastoral care, do not represent either the responsible, reliable parish pastor, nor the highly trained pastoral therapy specialist.

For those who want to become highly trained pastoral therapy specialists, not only is a great deal more theory needed than is represented in these pages, but also needed are years of competent supervision and personal psychotherapy. Twenty years ago, when the author entered the field, there were few programs that offered such a complete apprenticeship. The theoretical work took place in an academic setting, practicums were arranged at one's own initiative, and the psychotherapy was contracted privately. Today, however, there are many excellent training programs in pastoral therapy, approved by the American Association of Pastoral Counselors (Handbook 1976), which offer didactic theory, qualified supervision, personal psychotherapy, and some stipend, all in one setting.

Of the three aspects of training, theory, supervision, and personal psychotherapy, the supervisory experience generally is more important as a learning experience than didactic classes on theory, if the supervisor is an experienced and competent therapist. Persons recognized as competent supervisors are Fellows and Diplomates in the American Association of Pastoral Counselors. During a student's training, a variety of supervisors is advised, changed if possible every 12 months. It is also an advantage if some of the supervisors come from the disciplines of psychiatry, clinical psychology, and psychiatric social work, thus fostering some professional cross-fertilization. The supervision needs to consist of one individual and one group session each week, at least. A beginning pastoral therapist can learn from the mistakes and gains of other trainees through the presentation of case write-ups in group supervision. In selecting supervisors, some attention needs to be given to supervision in the main modes of therapy: individual, group, marriage, and family, so that the student experiences supervision in two modes, at least. It is unrealistic for a student to expect to be highly trained in all four modes, but it is reasonable to expect a competent pastoral therapist to be skilled in individual pastoral therapy and have some proficiency in one other mode.

The number of cases permitted a first-year supervisee will depend upon the supervisor and the setting in which the supervisor practices. Some centers, inundated by needy persons, allow a beginning therapist to take a large case load on a sink-or-swim basis. In such a situation, learning occurs but much of it can be negative learning which a later supervisor has to work on correcting. The preferred method is where the neophyte commences with one or two cases that are thoroughly discussed each supervisory session. In a suburban church setting the pastoral counseling center may have no other option but to carefully screen the cases given to a beginning student. Early work of the pastoral therapy student will consist of pastoral care, evaluating persons, referral work, and doing up to six months of supportive pastoral therapy in preparation for a client's intensive, uncovering pastoral therapy with another therapist. Students who don't have the patience for such work normally don't have the qualities to get them through the stalemates and tricky transferences that emerge during intensive, uncovering psychotherapy.

Before the end of the first year of training, it is hoped that the student has been able to prepare one person for intensive, uncovering pastoral therapy and then successfully refer that person to another therapist. In addition, it is hoped that one of the cases evaluated towards the end of the first year has been able to be assigned to the student for brief psychotherapy. If this case is going well at the beginning of the second year, the student is encouraged to have a second brief therapy case so that she or he does not become overinvested in one case, and so that the student can learn from comparing the two cases. At the same time evaluation, referrals, and preparation for therapy cases are continued. Whereas during the first year an hour of supervision is needed to cover an hour of clinical work, in the second year one hour of supervision covers four or five hours of clinical work without the feeling there is not enough supervisory time, if the student's work is steadily improving. Students in the first year are encouraged to present a tape or two so that the supervisor can get the "feel" of their work. Before a student is asked to present a tape for supervision she or he needs to regularly tape a client for some time so that the client becomes a little accustomed to the taping. Also, the student should not be aware of which specific tape will be asked for by her or his supervisor for supervisory purposes. Suddenly taping a pastoral therapy session without adequate preparation of the client just because the student has to present a tape for supervision, produces much rage in both client and student and an interaction atypical of the normal working alliance. Resistance to such a taping intrusion is reflected in the fact that more often than not tapes are of such poor quality they can scarcely be understood. If the supervisor persists in trying to hear the tapes she or he is placed in the position of having the student "interpret" what is being said! Taping, audio or video, should not occur unless time has been spent in supervision exploring the feelings of the student, and the student exploring the feelings of the client in therapy sessions.

The author has found it better to encourage supervisors to write up process notes of no more than a page on each therapy session. He leaves the listening tapes until after the student has had a chance to practice a little. Once a few tapes have been heard and discussed, supervision is conducted through a discussion of the regularly produced process notes. If a case ever produces a puzzling problem that can't be resolved through a discussion of process notes, after a time, tapes can be used to see if they can add a dimension that has been missed. In this way, taping is used for special problems and not for regular supervision. This is because process notes foster a sense of integration of the clinical material on each case in the mind of the trainee-therapist. It is this understanding, based on continual integration of the material of clinical sessions, which interacts with both the rational and unconscious parts of the client's mind, and fosters production of more material and further clarification of the client's unconscious fantasies and feelings. The use of process notes also fosters a practice, which with internalization, will enhance a personal form of supervision and will gradually make the presence of an external supervisor unnecessary. One sign of a student in difficulty with a case is where the process notes are neglected or show a complete lack of integration. It is another sign of a lack of progress if the student has to use tapes to make her or his process notes.

Students with two years of supervision behind them generally have met most of the formal requirements of supervision for applying to the American Association of Pastoral Counselors for member status. However, even when these formal requirements are met the student may not have mastered the skills necessary to function as a pastoral therapy specialist under supervision. A simple way to ascertain this is by the ability of the student to maintain four or five hours of casework with one session of supervision comfortably. Difficulties that occur in the cases of students generally center around the inability of the therapist to establish a working alliance with the client. The supervisory task is to explore with the therapist any possible reasons for this, especially any countertransference feelings on the part of the student that may be impeding the working alliance with the client. Generally, however, students whose clients seem to always be abruptly terminating with them, or who manifest countertransference acting-in to clients, will also have difficulty in maintaining a good working alliance with the supervisor. This lack of a learning alliance (the working alliance with the supervisor) needs to be given more careful attention than listening to tapes and obsessing about the minutiae of the interaction between therapist and client. Where sticky transference issues block a successful learning alliance, the student needs to tackle these in her or his personal psychotherapy.

In the author's opinion, personal psychotherapy is an absolute necessity for pastoral psychotherapists. Of the three components to learning pastoral therapy, didactic sessions, competent supervision, and personal psychotherapy, personal psychotherapy is where the best learning can take place. In this sense the therapist's first case is always herself or himself. The kind of therapy the pastoral therapist undertakes will depend on the kind of therapy she or he intends to practice. If the pastoral therapist is going to specialize in brief pastoral therapy, she or he needs to have therapy with an expert in brief pastoral therapy. If, on the other hand, the pastor intends to specialize in intensive, uncovering pastoral therapy, she or he needs to undergo intensive, uncovering psychotherapy twice or three times a week for three or four years, at least. Yet again, if the pastor is going to practice psychoanalysis, then she or he ought to be psychoanalyzed.

Intensive, uncovering pastoral therapy is usually a very expensive educational investment. Unless the student of pastoral therapy has a personal need for characterological change, she or he will generally elect to undergo brief pastoral therapy once a week for a year or so, so that she or he can conduct brief pastoral therapy under supervision. The student can then decide whether to learn intense, uncovering pastoral therapy if able to support herself or himself through conducting brief pastoral therapy. After graduating from a training program, the student is generally able to pay for her or his additional psychotherapy of an intensive nature. In deciding on intensive, uncovering pastoral therapy, it is important to select the most experienced therapist available, one who is known for her or his competence, for one's own psychotherapy. As is practiced with the student, so the student will practice with others because of the strong process of identification during the psychotherapy.

It is important to realize that those with the natural ability to conduct intensive, uncovering psychotherapy and have the commitment to see the prolonged training through to a successful completion, are few in number. This is true whether in the area of practice being considered they would be pastoral psychotherapists, psychiatrists, clinical psychologists or psychiatric social workers. Therefore, those pastors who can undertake this work should be encouraged to do so. However, need for pastors to conduct brief psychotherapy is equally important because the demand for this work is far more frequent than for the intensive, uncovering variety. Pastors who specialize in brief pastoral therapy fill an important niche in the care of persons, which should not be discounted both for the changes it helps facilitate and for the more serious problems it prevents. It is probably the rapid expansion of pastoral counseling centers, which mainly offer brief pastoral therapy, that accounts for the pastoral counseling movement's greatest contribution to the welfare of individuals, the church, and the country. At the same time, the presence of pastoral therapists in these centers conducting intensive, uncovering pastoral therapy is a reminder of both the strengths and limitations of the brief approach.

The claims of this text are not new. Pastoral therapy as a specialization of professional ministry has roots going back 50 years to the pioneering work of Anton Boisen, Chaplain of Worcester State Hospital, Massachusetts, and Richard Cabot, Professor of Clinical Medicine at Harvard Medical School (Thornton 1970). Boisen, the acknowledged grandfather of the modern pastoral therapy movement, through his own reactive schizophrenic experiences and through working with schizophrenic patients when they were considered poor therapeutic risks, was a staunch advocate of the therapeutic role of pastors. The foundation of the clinical pastoral education movement as a result of Boisen's example, laid a foundation in pastoral care that has, in turn, helped nourish the development of pastoral therapy specialists.

Support for the notion of pastoral therapy comes from other sources, as well. These include Freud himself who, in his correspondence with Pfister, a Protestant minister and "lay" analyst (Meng and Freud 1963) approves of Pfister's work. In response to Pfister's appeal to Freud to "cast a benevolent glance at the analytic cure of souls" (pastoral therapy), Freud replied: "It (lay analysis) is a piece of polemics written for a special occasion. Otherwise, I should certainly not have omitted the application of analysis to the cure of souls." Other support comes from Carroll Wise (1971) who was the successor to the chaplaincy position at Worcester when Boisen left and a recognized pioneer in the field by his own right. Further, Heije Faber (1975), on the Continent, says that "therapy and pastoral care are two different dimensions even if they encroach on each other."

Despite the support pastoral therapy has received from within the church and from the healing-helping professions, its development has also evoked considerable resistance. If pastoral therapists are dynamically oriented in theory, then such resistance to their work would not be unexpected. Resistance in the church took the form of theological questioning. In seeking to gain church acceptance for pastoral therapy, early writers gave considerable attention to the theological validity of the specialization they referred to as "counseling." The fact that the word counseling had to be used when healing as a therapeutic process was intended, as an indication that these writers were avoiding fostering any unnecessary resistance. Writers like Hiltner (1949), Johnson (1953), Oates (1959) and Wise (1951, 1966) wrote "apologetics" for their practice, using biblical, historical, and theological arguments. As one example, it was pointed out that the New Testament Greek word "soter," which was traditionally translated as "save." meant "heal" in many of the situations where it was used. (Richardson 1950).

Resistance from the healing-helping professions took the form of challenging the technical competence of pastoral therapists. This challenge from the secular direction led to the enforcement of higher standards for pastoral therapists than generally in force in the other healing professions. It has also led to the belief among pastoral therapists that by establishing a successful record of therapeutic work, pastoral therapists will eventually receive recognition as therapists from the mental health and insurance fields. One acknowledgment will take the form of third-party payments from insurance companies. This recognition is an addition to the generally held perception that pastors, through their pastoral care work, are important gatekeepers in the mental health field.

A question persistently raised by secular professionals is, "What is distinctive about pastoral therapy?" The question is reasonable enough, yet it has not been easy to answer because it raises questions about the identity of pastoral therapy specialists. In response to this question, some have insisted that pastoral therapists are distinctive because they utilize such special techniques as prayer and Bible reading, but because devout secular therapists are just as able to pray and read Scripture, these techniques, in themselves, don't give a satisfactory answer to the question of the distinctiveness of pastoral therapy. Others have tried to stress the importance of theological dogma for the uniqueness of pastoral therapy, with one writer seeing pastoral therapy as preaching to an audience of one (Thurneysen 1962) but this position has found very little support on the American scene.

Howard Clinebell (1966), in addressing himself to the question of pastoral "counseling's" uniqueness, takes a multifactored approach. He sees a combination of factors including 1) a broad liberal arts training which includes theology, philosophy, world religions, and ethics, 2) a symbolic role as a religious transference figure, 3) the setting in which the counseling takes place, 4) the methods the counselor uses, and 5) the goals of spiritual growth which are always present. His point is that while none of these factors by itself may make pastoral counseling unique, taken together they form a distinctive gestalt (wholeness) which is different from the sum of the parts (Bertalanffy 1968). Clinebell's argument, supported as it is by the general system theory, challenges a platonic view of uniqueness with its search for an irreducible core or distinctive essence. Clinebell's case for the unique contribution of pastoral counseling has considerable merit, but its widespread acceptance may have to await a broader understanding of the general system theory.

The position taken by the author is to stress the value of totemic figures conducting psychotherapy (Lee 1979). This is because totemic figures represent groups with which persons are closely identified, whether the totemic figures represent religious groups or causes such as those for blacks, women, or homosexuals. For those persons with strong feelings of bondedness to such causes or groups, there is often a rejection of persons from the out-group, irrespective of their competence. If they need psychotherapy, such persons will only accept a relationship with someone who is seen as a totemic representative of the group or cause. Thus, while universal therapists can function well with the majority of persons, totemic therapists, including pastoral therapists, are an absolute necessity for those with strong in-group loyalties. The uniqueness of the pastoral therapist as one type of totemic therapist is what is projected onto him by the strongly bonded members of her or his group or cause. Utilizing these magical projections in order to bring about an effective working alliance and challenge such persons to seek therapeutic change, is the unique position in which pastoral therapists repeatedly find themselves.

Pastoral therapists, then, form a small but significant group of healing-helping professionals. What impact pastoral therapy will play in the mental health of the nation is very much linked to future federal and state government legislation and third party insurance policies. Pastoral therapy will continue to exist as a specialized form of ministry because of its unique totemic role and because persons will always seek help from skilled pastors who are prepared to work for moderate fees, whether or not there is private insurance or government funding. But the issue of whether pastoral therapy remains a small specialization of ministry, or whether it emerges as a significant national force in the healing-helping field, is very much dependent on whether pastoral therapists are included in the decisions made in Washington over national health and the decisions made in the executive offices of major insurance companies, in the next few years. Licensing legislation at the state level could also effect the future of pastoral therapy. More importantly, pastoral therapy is dependent on the continued understanding, good will and support it has received from ecclesiastical officials, pastors, and lay persons.

Bibliography

Alexander, F. (1950) *Psychosomatic Medicine*. New York: Norton.

Auden, W. (1966) Prologue: The Birth of Architecture. In Hall, E. *The Hidden Dimension*. New York: Doubleday.

Bergin, A. (1970) The Deterioration Effect: A Reply to Braucht. *Journal of Abnormal Psychology*. 75: 300–302.

Berne, E. (1966) *The Games People Play*. London: Deutsch.

Berne, E. (1969) *Principles of Group Treatment*. New York: Oxford University Press.

Bertalanffy, L. von, (1968) *General System Theory*. New York: Braziller.

Brannigan, C. and Humphries, D. (1969) I See What You Mean. *New Scientist*, May 22: 406–408.

Braucht, G. (1970) The Deterioration Effect: A Reply to Bergen. *Journal of Abnormal Psychology*. 75, 293–299.

Brody, W. (1965) On the Dynamics of Narcissism, I. Externalization and Early Ego Development. *Psychoanalytic Study of the Child*. 20: 165–193.

Campbell, D. and Fisk, D. (1959) Convergent and Discriminant Validation by the Multitrait-Multimethod Matrix. *Psychological Bulletin*. 50, No 2: 81–105.

Cancro, R. (1968) Elopements from the C. F. Menninger Hospital. *Bulletin of the Menninger Clinic*, 32, No 4: 228–238.

Chessick, R. (1971) *Why Psychotherapists Fail*. New York: Science.

Chessick, R. (1974) *Technique and Practice of Intensive Psychotherapy*. New York: Aronson.

Christensen, C. (1952) Unpublished manuscript—Suggestions for Psychological Evaluations Prepared for Pastoral Counselors. (Modified from Masserman, J. Psychiatric Supplementation of the Medical History and Physical Examination. *Diseases of the Nervous System*. 23, No 8.

Christensen, C. (1958, 60, 61, 63) Occurance of Mental Illness in the Ministry. *The Journal of Pastoral Care*. 12, 14, 15, 17.

Christensen, C. (1966) The Minister—A psychotherapist? *Pastoral Psychology*. Oct: 31–39.

Clinebell, H. (1966) *Basic Types of Pastoral Counseling*. New York: Abingdon.

Cohn M. B., Baker G., Cohen R. S., et al: (1954) An intensive study of twelve cases of manic-depressive psychosis. *Psychiatry* 17: 103–137.

Coltrera J. T., Ross N. (1967) Freud's Psychoanalytic Techniques—1923 in *Psychoanalytic Techniques* by Wolman B. B. N.Y., Basic.

Denenberg, V. and Karas, G. (1962) Reported by Scott, J. in "Critical Periods of Behavioral Development". *Science.* 138: 949–958.

Douglas, J. (1970) *Behavior Today.* 23.

Draper, E., Meyer, G., Parzen, Z., and Samuelson, G. (1965) On the Diagnostic Value of Religious Ideation. *Archives of General Psychiatry.* 13: 202–207.

Erikson, E. (1950) *Childhood and Society.* New York: Norton.

Faber, H. (1975) *Psychology of Religion.* Philadelphia: Westminster.

Fenichel, O. (1945) *Psychoanalytic Theory of Neurosis.* New York: Norton.

Fieve, R., Rosenthal, D., and Brill, H. (1975) *Genetic Research in Psychiatry.* Baltimore: John Hopkins University Press.

Flarsheim, A. (1972) Treatability. In *Tactics and Techniques in Psychoanalytic Therapy* by Giovacchini, P. New York: Science.

Florell, J. (1971) *Crisis Intervention in Orthopedic Surgery.* Unpublished doctoral dissertation, Northwestern University. Evanston, Ill.

Freud, A. (1965) *Normality and Pathology in Childhood.* New York: International Universities Press.

Freud, A. (1966) *The Ego and the Mechanisms of Defense.* New York: International Universities Press.

Freud, S. (1909) A Case of Obsessional Neurosis. In *Collected Papers.* III, New York: Basic, 1959.

Fromm-Reichmann, F. (1950) *Principles of Intensive Psychotherapy.* Chicago: University of Chicago Press.

Gill, M. (1951) Ego Psychology and Psychotherapy. *Psychoanalytic Quarterly.* 20: 62–71.

Green, H., (1964) *I Never Promised You a Rose Garden.* New York: Holt Rinehart and Winston.

Greene, B. (1970) *A Clinical Approach to Marital Problems.* Springfield Ill.: Thomas.

Greene, B., Lustig, N. and Lee, R. (1976) Marital Therapy Where One Spouse has a Primary Affective Disorder. *The American Journal of Psychiatry.* 133, No 7: 827–830.

Greenson, R. (1965) Working Alliance and Transference Neurosis. *Psychoanalytic Quarterly.* 34: 155–181.

Greenson, R. (1968) *The Technique and Practice of Psychoanalysis.* New York: International Universities Press.

Gurin, G., Veroff, J., and Feld, S. (1960) *Americans View Their Mental Health.* New York: Basic.

Handbook of the American Association of Pastoral Counselors. (1976) (See also the Directory of Members. Both Handbook and Directory can be obtained from A.A.P.C., 3 West 29th St., New York: New York, 10001).

Hess, E. (1958) Imprinting in Animals. *Scientific American*. March: 81–90.

Hiltner, S. (1949) *Pastoral Counseling*. New York: Abingdon.

Hiltner, S. and Colston G. (1961) *The Context of Pastoral Counseling*. New York: Abingdon.

Hovland, C., Janis, I. and Kelley, H. (1953) *Communication and Persuasion*. New Haven: Yale University Press.

Jackson, E. (1975) *Parish Counseling*. New York: Aronson.

Jensen, J. (1964) Faulty Management of Dependency Problems. *Journal of Pastoral Care*. 18: 37–40.

Johnson, P. (1953) *Psychology of Pastoral Care*. New York: Abingdon.

Kernberg, O. et al, (1972) Psychotherapy and Psychoanalysis. *Bulletin of the Menninger Clinic*. 36. 1–198.

Klink, T. (1962) The Referral: Helping People Focus Their Needs. *Pastoral Psychology*. 13, No 129: 10–15.

Klink, T. (1965) *Depth Perspectives in Pastoral Work*. Englewood Cliffs, N.J.: Prentice-Hall.

Kohut, H. (1971) *The Analysis of the Self*. New York: International Universities Press.

Kubler-Ross, E. (1969) *On Death and Dying*. New York: Macmillan.

Langs, R. (1973) (1974) *The Technique of Psychoanalytic Psychotherapy*. Vols I. and II New York: Aronson.

Langs, R. (1976) *The Bipersonal Field*. New York: Aronson.

Lee, R. (1979) Totemic Therapy, *Journal of Religion and Health*, Vol 18, No 1, 21–28.

Lewin, K. (1970) *Brief Psychotherapy*. St. Louis: Warren H. Green.

Levinson, H. (1962) *Men, Management and Mental Health*. Cambridge, Mass: Harvard University Press.

Lindemann, E. (1944) Symptomatology and Management of Acute Grief. *American Journal of Psychiatry*. 101: 141–148.

Lindner, R. (1955) *The Fifty Minute Hour*. New York: Rinehart.

Mackinnon, R. and Michels, R. (1971) *The Psychiatric Interview*. Philadelphia: Saunders.

Mahler, M., Pine, F., Bergmann, A., (1975) *The Psychological Birth of the Human Infant*, N.Y., Basic.

Meng, H. and Freud, E. (1963) *Psychoanalysis and Faith* (Letters of S. Freud and O. Pfister) New York: Basic.

Menninger, K. (1958) *Theory of Psychoanalytic Technique*. New York: Basic.

Menninger, K. (1963) *The Vital Balance*. New York: Viking.

Mitchell, K. (1972) Tacit Contracts. *Pastoral Psychology*. 23: 7–18.

Moss, D. and Lee, R. (1975) Homogamous and Heterogamous Marriages. *International Journal of Psychoanalytic Psychotherapy*. 5: 395–411.

Nygren, A. (1953) *Agape and Eros*. Philadelphia: Westminster.

Oates, W. (1959) *An Introduction to Pastoral Counseling*. Nashville: Broadman.

Pattison, E. (1965) Transference and Countertransference in Pastoral Care. *The Journal of Pastoral Care*. 19, Winter: 193–202.

Richardson, A. (1950) *A Theological Wordbook of the Bible*. London: S.C.M.

Roche Report (1968) *Frontiers in Clinical Psychiatry*. Dec.

Rosenzweig, E. (1941) Minister and Congregation—A Study in Ambivalence. *Psychoanalytic Review*. 28: 218–227.

Ruesch, J. (1961) *Therapeutic Communication*. New York: Norton.

Segal, H. (1963) Melanie Klein's Technique. In Wolman, B. *Psychoanalytic Techniques*. New York: Basic.

Sheafer, D. (1968) Staying in Bed as Resistance to Treatment. *Bulletin of the Menninger Clinic*. 32, No 4: 219–227.

Singer, E. (1970) *Key Concepts in Psychotherapy*. New York: Basic.

Smith, J. (1973) *Behavior Today*. March 10.

Sullivan, H. (1954) *The Psychiatric Interview*. New York: Norton.

Tauber, E. and Green, M. (1959) *Prelogical Experience*. New York: Basic.

Thornton, E. (1970) *Professional Education for Ministry*. New York: Abingdon.

Thurneysen E. (1962) *A Theology of Pastoral Care*. Richmond: John Knox.

Toman, W. (1961) *Family Constellation*. New York: Springer.

White, A. (1953) The Patient Sits Down. *Psychosomatic Medicine*. 15: 256–257.

Williamson, D. (1967) A Study of Selective Inhibition of Aggression by Church Members. *The Journal of Pastoral Care*. 21, Dec: 193–208.

Winnicott, D. (1966) *The Maturational Processes and the Facilitating Environment*. New York: International University Press.

Winokur, G. (1969) *Manic Depressive Illness*. St. Louis: Mosby.

Wise, C. (1951) *Pastoral Counseling*. New York: Harper.

Wise, C. (1966) *The Meaning of Pastoral Care*. New York: Harper.

Wise, C. (1971) *The Institutional Ministry, Retrospect and Prospect*. Unpublished address to the 25th anniversary lunceon of the College of Chaplains of the American Protestant Hospital Association, Denver, Col. March 15.

Wolberg, L. (1954) *The Technique of Psychotherapy*. Parts I and II. New York: Grune and Stratton.

Young, R. and Meiburg, A. (1960) *Spiritual Therapy*. London: Hodder and Stoughton.

Zeligs, M. (1957) Acting In. *Journal of the American Psychoanalytic Association*. 5: 685–706.

Zetzel, E. (1956) Current Concepts of Transference. *International Journal of Psychoanalysis*. 37: 369–376.